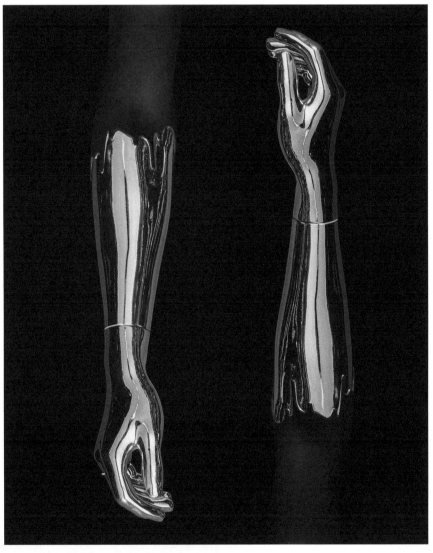

HANS BOODT.
MANNEQUINS

PARIS BLACK COPPER COLLECTION
WWW.HANSBOODT.COM

It began with a spark... it has burned for 333 years.

The difference is **Gaggenau.**

In 1683, from the depths of the Black Forest, a flame sprang to life and the age of the industrial craftsmanship began. From the same process that saw a forge emerge, the invention of the Badenia bicycle and the introduction of the combi-steam oven to the private kitchen, we have always imagined what could be. Then built it.

333 years of working with metal is an achievement only few can claim. It exposes a success that has crossed time, distance and cultures. Gaggenau is not just a kitchen appliance; it is the soul of a home and it is this passion that has been 333 years in the making.

For more information, please visit www.gaggenau.com.

DESIGN PORTRAIT.

Michel Club, seat system designed by Antonio Citterio. www.bebitalia.com

Vanrikxoort Agenturen - Rene Van Rikxoort T. +31 627095888 - vra05@xs4all.nl

US Patent n° US D 709,637 S, EU registration n° 002024612

terzani.com

Mizu, *Flowing Light*
design Nicolas Terzani

TERZANI
LA LUCE PENSATA

Photo Dennis Lo

Arboit Limited sends office workers into the clouds on page 090.

CONTENTS

Photo Noah Kalina

Photo Lukas Renlund

On page 039, Ikea explores the future of living through its signature dish: meatballs.

Snarkitecture singles out key moments in its career on page 073.

Standard white tiles signal unrefined food for AKZ's Orang+Utan restaurant on page 086.

Photo Lesha Yanchenkov

Photo Juliane Eirich

On page 130, Vittorio Radice shares his in-store secrets.

Thonet's All Seasons collection follows a playful approach to outdoor furniture on page 201.

— FRAME LAB —
Colour
Chromatic approaches to health-boosting interiors
139

Photo Erin O'Keefe, courtesy of Denny Gallery, NYC

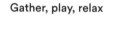

A video featuring this logo allow you to view extra content in the digital magazine

FRAME IS PUBLISHED
SIX TIMES A YEAR BY

Frame Publishers
Laan der Hesperiden 68
NL-1076 DX Amsterdam
T +31 20 423 3717
F +31 20 428 0653
frame@frameweb.com
frameweb.com

Editorial

EDITOR IN CHIEF
Robert Thiemann – **RT**

MANAGING EDITOR
Tracey Ingram – **TI**

EDITORS
Floor Kuitert – **FK**
Maria Elena Oberti – **MO**

EDITORIAL INTERN
Christian Walters – **CW**

COPY EDITORS
InOtherWords (D'Laine Camp,
Donna de Vries-Hermansader)

DESIGN DIRECTOR
Barbara Iwanicka

GRAPHIC DESIGNERS
Vincent Hammingh
Cathelijn Kruunenberg

TRANSLATION
InOtherWords (Maria van Tol,
Donna de Vries-Hermansader)

**CONTRIBUTORS
TO THIS ISSUE**
Alice Blackwood – **AB**
Nicola Bozzi – **NB**
Will Georgi – **WG**

Grant Gibson – **GG**
Lauren Grieco – **LG**
Kanae Hasegawa – **KH**
Ronald Hooft – **RH**
Adrian Madlener – **AM**
Melanie Mendelewitsch – **MM**
Kim van der Meulen – **KvdM**
Enya Moore – **EM**
Shonquis Moreno – **SM**
James Myers – **JM**
Jonathan Openshaw – **JO**
Jill Pope – **JP**
Anna Sansom – **AS**
Jane Szita – **JS**
Suzanne Wales – **SW**
Anne van der Zwaag – **AvdZ**

WEB EDITOR
Lauren Grieco
lauren@frameweb.com

COVER
Image Lorenzo Vitturi

LITHOGRAPHY
Edward de Nijs

PRINTING
Grafisch Bedrijf Tuijtel
Hardinxveld-Giessendam

Publishing

DIRECTORS
Robert Thiemann
Rudolf van Wezel

**SALES AND MARKETING
DIRECTOR**
Margreet Nanning
margreet@frameweb.com

BRAND MANAGER
Hanneke Stuij
hanneke@frameweb.com

**DISTRIBUTION
AND LOGISTICS**
Nick van Oppenraaij
nick@frameweb.com

FINANCE
Cedric Isselt
cedric@frameweb.com

Pearl Yssel
pearl@frameweb.com

Advertising

SALES MANAGERS
Nikki Brandenburg
nikki@frameweb.com

Sarah Maisey
sarahmaisey@frameweb.com

**ADVERTISING
REPRESENTATIVES
Italy**
Studio Mitos
Michele Tosato
T +39 0422 894 868
michele@studiomitos.it

Turkey
Titajans
Hilmi Zafer Erdem
T +90 212 257 76 66
titajans@titajans.com

**LICENCE HOLDERS
Korea**
Tong Yang Media Co. Ltd.
Young Lee
T +82 70 8169 6013
framekorea@gmail.com

QUERIES
service@frameweb.com

BOOKSTORE DISTRIBUTORS
Frame is available at sales
points worldwide.
Please see frameweb.com/
magazines/where-to-buy.

**Frame (USPS No: 019-372)
is published bimonthly by
Frame Publishers NL and
distributed in the USA by
Asendia USA, 17B South
Middlesex Ave., Monroe, NJ
08831. Periodicals postage
paid at New Brunswick,
NJ, and additional mailing
offices.**

**Postmaster: send address
changes to *Frame*, 701C
Ashland Ave., Folcroft,
PA 19032.**

ISSN FRAME: 1388-4239

Subscribe

Regular subscription
From €99
**Introductory 1-year
subscription**
From €79
Student subscription
From €69

Visit frameweb.com/subscribe
for more options or e-mail us at
service@frameweb.com.

Back issues
Buy online at store.frameweb.com

Frame 108

Frame 107

Frame 106

Frame 105

X-Code

Design: Daniel Figueroa

www.dauphin.de

Dauphin HumanDesign® Group

True Colours

For this issue, cover artist Lorenzo Vitturi abstracted everyday objects using natural pigments and spices.

Cover artist Lorenzo Vitturi explores the transformative nature of pure pigments for this issue's colour theme.

WORDS *Maria Elena Oberti*

How did you approach the brief?
LORENZO VITTURI: Colour plays a major role in my work, so I was very excited to receive this commission. The sculptures you see in this series are composed of different things I found around my neighbourhood in East London, where I live and work. My idea was to take these seemingly random objects out of their natural context and infuse them with new meaning using colour.

Can you take us through your process?
My process can be best described as a combination of construction and improvisation. I always start off with some rough sketches. These simple drawings set the overall mood for my compositions and help me understand what shapes I need to look for during my research. The process I used for the cover was very free; the only constraints were the physical limitations of my neighbourhood. I went to shops, junkyards and flea markets in search of intriguing materials and shapes. Once satisfied with my collection, I took the objects back to my studio and made

a final selection. I then abstracted the objects using pigments and spices.

The pigments I use in my work are pure, like those in classical painting. I believe pure pigments are the strongest and most emotive way to experience colour. Once I've finalized the palette, I start building and documenting the process through photography.

How do you decide which objects will work? What makes an object appropriate for this type of composition? My work is driven mostly by instinct and the senses, which often inform my selection of materials. It's impossible to know what the street will offer. What I look for are objects with rich and complex shapes. I base my selection on the objects that are most interesting from a sensorial point of view.

When did you start experimenting with colour? I started exploring and working with colour during my studies in Venice. At the time, painting was my main medium, and I was heavily

influenced by the works of Venetian Renaissance masters such as Giorgione and Bellini. I later applied this knowledge to my set designs for Rome's Cinecittà, where I adopted the role of a still-life painter, creating realistic representations of natural materials such as marble and stone for film, using colour and traditional painting techniques. That's when I started to work with pigments in their natural form.

Which of the Frame Lab topics inspired you most? I was mainly inspired by the connection between colour and the senses or, more specifically, the idea that colour acts as a stimulus for the senses. It's something I think about a lot in my work, and the concept spoke to me immediately. Colour is ephemeral. Our perception of it is constantly changing. I am intrigued by the subjective quality of colour and the way in which our senses, moods and environments influence how we engage with and understand it. ✕
lorenzovitturi.com

Design. Quality. Vision.
bulthaup passion comes alive when machines have reached
their limits and a keen human eye and skilled hands are needed
for completing your kitchen. www.bulthaup.com

bulthaup

On the wall of our dining room are six graphic works that I hung there in a free-form composition. They differ quite a bit in terms of subject matter, size and maker. One of the six is an abstract, man-sized, silk-screen print; another is a framed album cover; and a third features a large Z-shaped object. Black and white dominate five of the images. Orange appears in four, and that's about it as far as colour is concerned. Composition and homogeneity of the few colours used generate a calm state of mind as your eyes move across the wall. When you look at the works one by one, however, you're struck by huge contrasts and the enormous scope of expressivity.

For years I've been looking at that wall with great pleasure. Every day. And now I know why. Colour expert Hilary Dalke offers an explanation on page 141: 'When you're in a single-colour environment,' she says, 'you'll soon become totally unaware of the colour. Contrast is everything.' If you also know that orange is a warm hue associated with bliss and that it sends a strong message, you'll understand why I leave the office and hurry home for lunch every day. (I enjoy the meals, too.)

Contrast is everything

Apparently, I gave my dining room a good vibe, albeit intuitively. Designers tasked with the interiors of hospitals, pharmacies and fitness clubs would be wise to combine intuition with an in-depth knowledge of the job at hand, says Dalke. She thinks describing red as warm and blue as cool is much too simple. In the built environment, colours have an effect only in combinations that are rich in contrast. Painting your baby daughter's room pink, for instance, doesn't make much sense: without contrast, neither mother nor child will notice the colour as time passes. Applying colour intelligently, though, can lead to striking results. Dalke herself achieved a drastic reduction in suicide attempts among prison inmates by introducing subtle patterns of colour to the institution's tiled showers.

In this issue, we get enthusiastic about the positive impact that colour has on wellbeing. We look at experimental uses of colour in a pharmacy, and at vibrant interactive installations in a children's hospital. For those of you who need more inspiration than application, we offer two provocative visual essays intended to stimulate the creative juices.

I'm writing this in my office at Frame. Behind me is another wall filled with graphic work. A wall that seldom catches my eye – and now I know why. Too many hues, too little contrast. All those images merge to make a nondescript chaos of colour.

So, time to head home for lunch. ×

Robert Thiemann, Editor in Chief
robert@frameweb.com

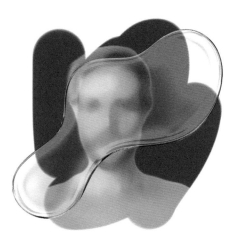

'I enjoy researching projects that involve interdisciplinary, concept-driven efforts. The process is always similar, but the change in perspective opens up worlds of possibilities for art and space'

James 'JD' Myers is an American designer living and working in Amsterdam. A trained architect specializing in retail experience and conceptual design, he strives to push social boundaries through the use of spatial design and architecture. Possessing a passion for minimalist aesthetics and a curiosity for the fringe of society, he explores social norms and perceptions through writing, art and architecture. Myers contributed to this issue's Seeds.

'Stéphane Malka applied elements of his broader philosophy for urban sustainability while creating an office that doesn't look like an office'

Jill Pope, who lives and works in Paris, is an Australian journalist and editor who describes herself as 'a voracious consumer of design, food and urban culture'. Besides writing for *Frame* and other top-notch publications, Pope is working towards her postgraduate degree in urban anthropology, researching the people and places that make up our cities. For this issue, she examined the striking Adyax workplace by Stéphane Malka.

'I was so captured by the concept of the decaying papier-mâché egg that I decided to use it as the backdrop for the shoot. I think it's a perfect representation of the ideas and spirit that drive Ghaith&Jad'

Born in Beirut in 1968, Lebanese photographer **Joe Kesrouani** began experimenting with painting and photography at the age of 14. He fled his war-torn city in 1990 to pursue a degree at the renowned École Nationale Supérieure d'Architecture de Paris la Villette. Ten years later, Kesrouani published *Monochromes*, a retrospective work featuring images captured between 1989 and 2009. Currently living and working in Beirut, Kesrouani has mounted solo exhibitions at home and abroad. For this issue, Kesrouani visited Beirut duo Ghaith&Jad.

'It was a pleasure to speak to Erwan and Ronan and to hear about their most significant encounters and influences'

Melanie Mendelewitsch is an independent French journalist and novelist based in Paris. Her first book was released in 2008, and she is working on a second publication. In her role as journalist, Mendelewitsch covers culture and social affairs for the French editions of *GQ*, *Vanity Fair*, *Grazia*, *Glamour* and *Slate*. She also contributes to international magazines, such as the US edition of *Vanity Fair*, *The Daily Beast*, *New York Observer*, *Paper* and *V Magazine*. For *Frame* 109, Mendelewitsch interviewed French designers Erwan and Ronan Bouroullec for 'What I've Learned'.

'It was five days before Christmas when we visited Snarkitecture, and we felt the pre-holiday chaos in their studio. Alex and Daniel were a great team to shoot – they have such great chemistry'

Born and raised in Japan, photographer **Kyoko Hamada** holds a degree in photography and painting from New York's Pratt Institute. With over ten years of experience, Hamada has seen her work featured in international publications such as *The New Yorker*, *The Atlantic* and *The Wall Street Journal*. Other clients include Vitra, Uniqlo and Kärcher. Her latest photo series, *I Used to be You*, received the grand prize at the LensCulture International Exposure Awards. Hamada's images of the Snarkitecture boys were taken at their Brooklyn studio.

'I studied architecture and design before going into photography and was very familiar with the Bouroullecs' work. It was really exciting to finally meet and photograph the brothers in their studio'

Valentin Fougeray is a French photographer based in Paris. Since graduating from visual-arts school Gobelins in 2014, Fougeray has worked with numerous prestigious institutions, magazines and brands. Inspired by the objects and people that surround him, Fougeray merges sensibility with imagination in his images. For *Frame* 109, Fougeray shot the portraits of Erwan and Ronan Bouroullec.

imagination by you

Now we launch new elmosoft colours.
Order your leather samples now!

www.elmoleather.com

leather by elmo®

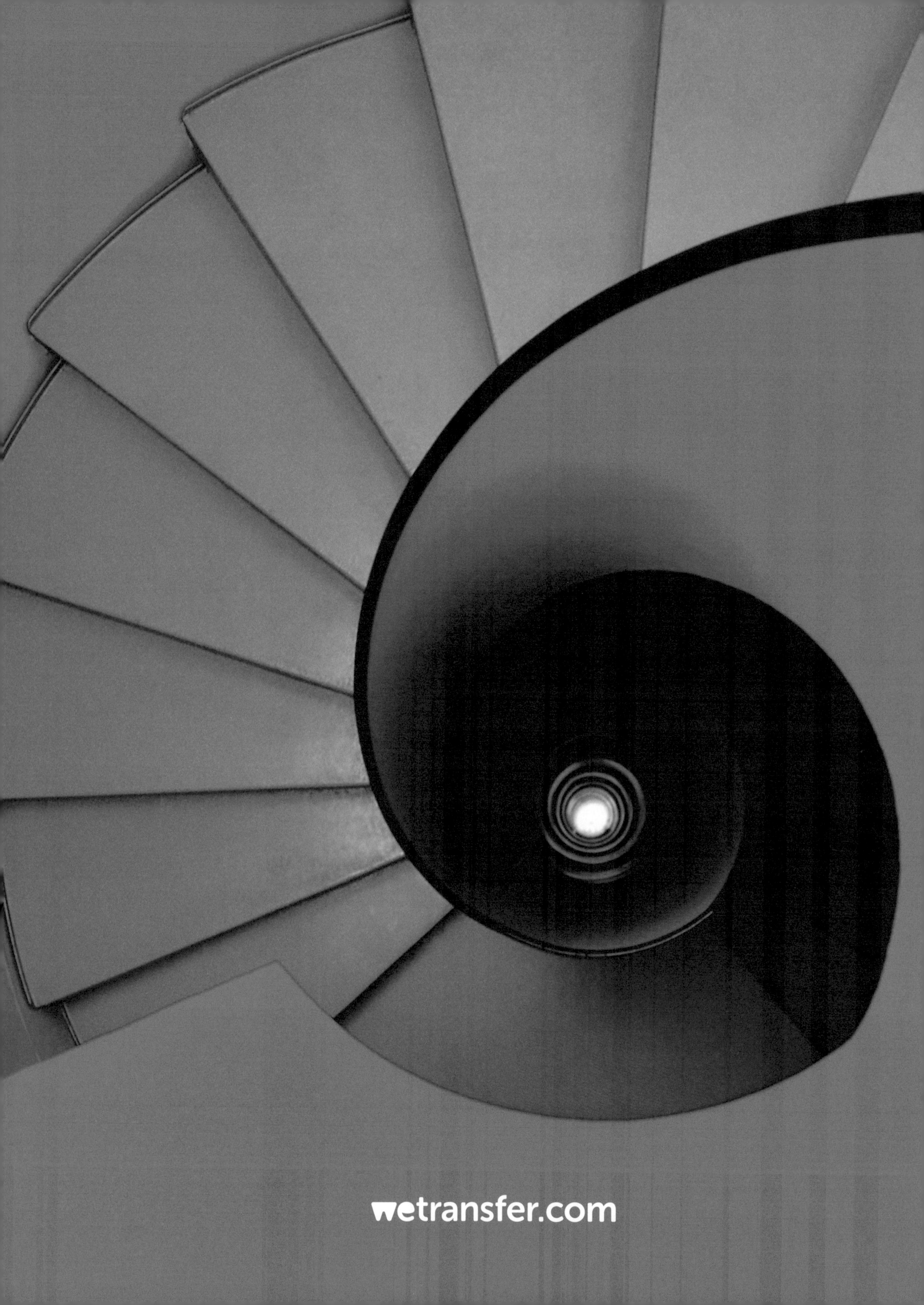
wetransfer.com

Seeds

Designers <u>relive their youth</u>. Ikea explores the <u>future of living</u>. <u>Customized cocktails</u> are served by a bartending robot. Kitchens become territories for <u>home-made medication</u>. Design Miami exhibitors <u>repurpose mundane materials</u>. All this and more is bubbling on the fringes of the great indoors.

State of Matter reveals the unexpected phenomena lying dormant in flour and H$_2$O

JUST ADD WATER

The One Particle by David Mergelmeyer and Virginia Clasen

Straddling scientific research and materials transformation, State of Matter – a workshop developed by Clemens Winkler, Stefan Schwabe and Jannis Hülsen – showed the reactive potential concealed in seemingly ordinary substances. The workshop, held at the 2015 edition of Vorspiel Transmediale in Berlin, explored the surreal through tangible experiments. The team examined the unexpected phenomena that can occur by combining standard kitchen flour and water from the bathroom tap. As participants witnessed the various complex states of such basic materials, they experienced the collective's interest in dimension, perspective and the deconstruction of matter. — CW

clemenswinkler.com
stschwabe.com
jannishuelsen.com

Holy Shit by Jérôme Gautier and Gosia Lehmann

FRAM3 Watch surreal footage of water interacting with flour in the digital magazine

Experiencing Matter States

LEFROY BROOKS

Come to the 55th year of wow in design.

Salone
del Mobile
Milano

12/17 April 2016
Fiera Milano, Rho.

EuroCucina, International Kitchen Furniture Exhibition/FTK,
Technology For the Kitchen. International Bathroom Exhibition.
International Furnishing Accessories Exhibition. SaloneSatellite.

Photo Studio Tomás Saraceno

UP
AND
AWAY

Tomás Saraceno's topical intervention at the Grand Palais in Paris calls for a sustainable future

They say timing is everything. Launched to coincide with the 2015 United Nations Climate Change Conference in Paris, *Aeroscene*, an installation by Tomás Saraceno, saw visitors in the foyer of the Grand Palais gazing up at giant air-filled globes. In what Saraceno hopes will be the longest emission-free journey around the earth, the

globes are set to make the trip fuelled only by the heat of the sun and infrared radiation from the earth. This flight is just the beginning, however. The plastic inflatables are part of a larger and more ambitious project that the Argentinian artist has been working on for years. Searching for answers to the world's 'current and troublesome dependency on fossil and hydrocarbon fuels and pollution', Saraceno is initiating community workshops and social media campaigns as part of his mission to raise awareness of the dangers inherent in climate change. — EM

tomassaraceno.com

MORNING GLORY

Sabine Marcelis's light sculptures emulate the break of dawn

Holding all that comes within a single moment of the day – sky, daylight, clouds – Sabine Marcelis's Dawn is a series of luminaires whose cast-resin forms are embedded with neon tubes and highlighted by what Marcelis calls a fleeting 'riot of colours'. Each piece plays with the relationship between translucency and opacity. Introduced by Brussels gallery Victor Hunt at Design Miami 2015, the Rotterdam-based designer's latest foray into colour and shape builds on her previous Voie Light Series #1. The new collection employs the same concept – 'the subtle manipulation of colour and its intersection with light' – while pushing scale and material to new heights. Ranging from relatively small yet sturdy cylindrical rods to larger rectilinear objects, the Dawn series demonstrates the maker's mastery of cast resin and its myriad possibilities. — AM

sabinemarcelis.com

Photo Lee Wei Swee, courtesy of Victor Hunt Gallery

DARK MATTER

Design Miami exhibitors repurpose mundane materials

① Lex Pott preserves Belgian bluestone offcuts in a furniture collection, while Calico applies the material's pigments to wallpaper.

Photo Oliver Staiano (product) / Lauren Coleman (background)

② With 3D printing and explosion welding, Janne Kyttanen fuses volcanic rock and metal to make a sculptural table.

Photo Sayoko Lynn

Photo Loek Blonk, courtesy of Chamber NYC Ltd.

As the art world flooded America's famed tropical metropolis with a heavy schedule of events, discerning tastemakers gathered to discover what the December edition of Design Miami had to offer. The now well-ingrained limited-edition tradition – setting the tone with top craftsmanship and innovative materials – finds itself at the forefront of an industry in search of authenticity and clear expression.

Among a diverse array of ceramics, glassware, jewellery – and an outdoor Greek-inspired forum mounted by Airbnb – a select number of galleries and talented young designers stole the show, all with an eye to upcycling mundane materials through new applications. More than simply a group of objects dark in complexion, their striking pieces played on complex textures available in nature and made possible by technology.

New York platform The Future Perfect married the genius of handmade Calico wallpaper and the prowess of Lex Pott ① in an installation in which Calico painters applied colour to a linen substrate *during* the event, in response

to Fragments, the Dutchman's furniture collection. Juxtaposing the natural roughness of Belgian bluestone with the clean geometry of polished glass, Pott's pieces gave rise to dramatic landscapes.

Newer galleries included Beijing-based All, which made its mark with Metsidian by Finnish designer Janne Kyttanen ②. Combining metal and volcanic rock, the table appears to move forward like the passage of time. Kyttanen achieved the duality of the structure, which features copper or chrome mesh and a rather prehistoric form, with the aid of 3D printing and explosion welding.

Set between booths at the fair, a series of Design Curio presentations shed commercial constraints to provide curated forays into contemporary culture. Juan Garcia Mosqueda's New York gallery, Chamber, brought Dutch designer Quintus Kropholler ③ to light. For his Black Gold series, Kropholler collected cast-off chunks of asphalt concrete from the street and transformed them into benches, side tables, bookstands and vases. His interest

③ Quintus Kropholler highlights the aesthetic potential of asphalt with a 16-legged stool.

lies in the haptic and aesthetic qualities of the material, which is a by-product of the petroleum industry. At the request of Chamber, he added a stool, a mirror and a divider screen to his collection for the show in Miami. — AM

calicowallpaper.com
lexpott.nl
jannekyttanen.com
quintuskropholler.com

TOY STORY

Fanciful and free: childlike thinking is something most grown-ups wish they'd never lost, especially those working in the creative industry. The rise of adult-only ball pits and therapeutic colouring books signals a growing desire to relive our careless youth. Play not only offers a retreat from reality, but also clears the mind of stress and – a designer's must – boosts the imagination. – FK

1

2

Photos Lee Thompson

Photo Daantje Bons

①   Shane Campbell Gallery provided a venue for Lisa Williamson's 'quasi-relatable' chromatic sculptures, which were part of her exhibition: Dimensional Shapes in Space.

②   A result of Jolene Carlier's imagination, Popcorn Monsoon embodies the joy of watching little kernels burst into a favourite snack.

Photo Asaf Gam Hacohen

5

3

4

Photos courtesy of J.W. Anderson

③ The two red Lego pieces that make up Talia Sari's Levo heart necklace function as both pendant and clasp.

④ Wild facial paint and sweaters with curved shoulders characterize J.W. Anderson's Pre-Autumn 2016 collection.

⑤ Tubo, a spatial installation by Mathery Studio that appeared at the IN77 shopping mall during Hangzhou International Design Week, invited kids to colour the space in 3D.

PLAY OFFERS A RETREAT FROM REALITY

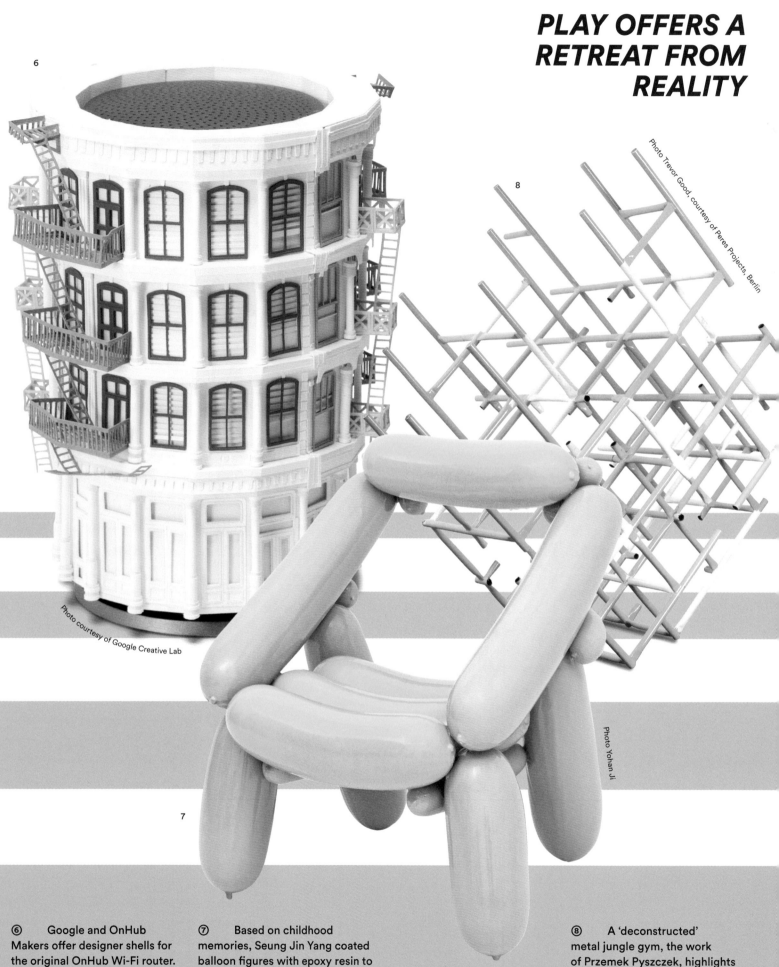

6

8

Photo Trevor Good, courtesy of Peres Projects, Berlin

Photo courtesy of Google Creative Lab

Photo Yohan Ji

7

⑥   Google and OnHub Makers offer designer shells for the original OnHub Wi-Fi router. Among them is an elaborate façade by Papersmith.

⑦   Based on childhood memories, Seung Jin Yang coated balloon figures with epoxy resin to make a vivid set of Blowing Chairs and Stools.

⑧   A 'deconstructed' metal jungle gym, the work of Przemek Pyszczek, highlights the Polish-Canadian artist's *Playground Structures*.

SCINTILLATING SPHERE

Onformative's audiovisual installation animates a dimmed room

Contemporary life often requires immediate reactions from one type of technology or another, but what about the spaces that surround us and the art that occupies those spaces? Straight out of a sci-fi movie, a glowing sphere suspended in a darkened room responds to its environment through light, modulated sound and colour. The reference is to *Anima Iki*, a sculptural installation conjured by German studio Onformative, which produces digital art and design. Illuminated from within, the interactive globe acts and reacts to viewers in a dynamic exchange of what the makers call 'soundscape and visuals'. Unlike static works of art, *Anima Iki* offers visitors a completely immersive sensory experience. — JM

onformative.com

FRAME EXHIBITION

WHAT'S THE MATTER?
Design for a phygital world

Milan Design Week 2016
12 – 17 April

La Posteria, Via Giuseppe Sacchi 5/7
Brera District

events.frameweb.com

POWERED BY

RICOH
imagine. change.

net design raffaello galiotto

Nnardi®

YOUR OUTDOOR LIVING

Photos Nicolas Genta

ÉCAL design graduates Aurélie Mathieu and Charlotte Sunnen, a duo known as Grande, share an aim to remove traditional constraints typically associated with rigid materials by developing projects that demonstrate the opportunities possible in the oldest of resources: stone. Their most recent offering, 6×6 Part 2, is a progressive series of furniture that features laminated stone. A continuation of the designers' debut collection, 6×6 Part 1, the new pieces – which began as discarded remnants of Marquina marble sourced from the Gros-Dérudet factory in Lyon – are a console, a table and a lamp. The furniture is composed of 6-x-6-cm marble battens whose sandwiched layers are glued together with a stark red adhesive. Grande shows that recycled leftovers can be strong enough to make large structures *and* to please connoisseurs of 21st-century aesthetics. Part 3? Yes please. — **CW**

grande-edition.ch

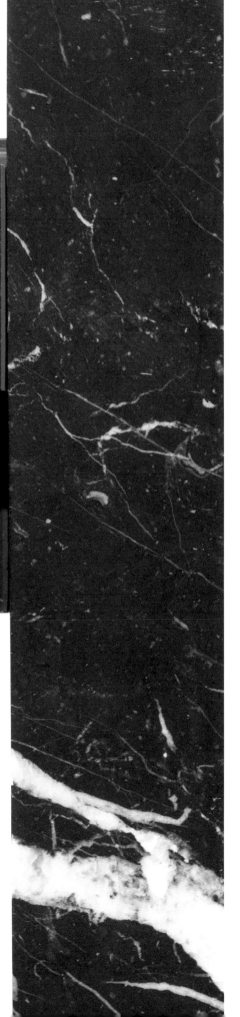

STONE SANDWICH

A Swiss-based design duo optimizes a classic material for modern production

DOMESTIC DRUGS

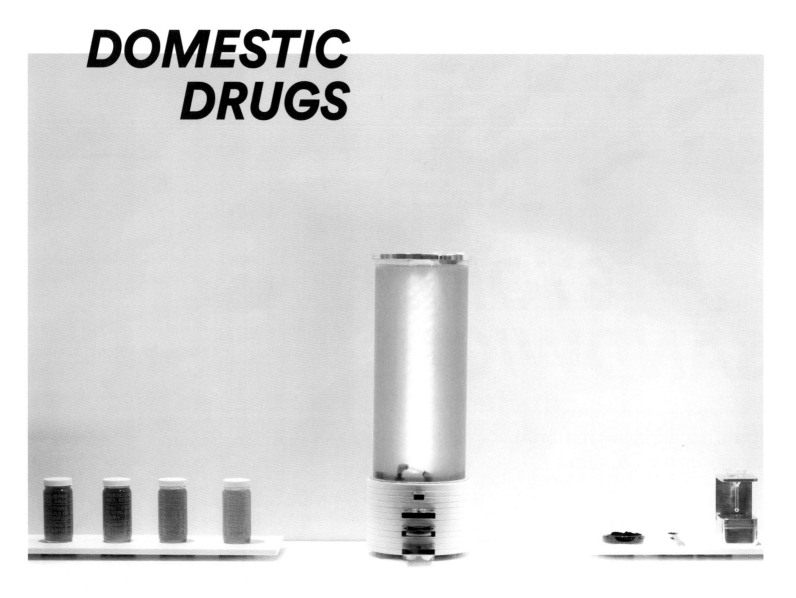

Genetic engineering holds promise for home-made medication

Martin Shkreli's rise to notoriety – among other vices, he hiked the price of life-saving drugs by more than 5,000 per cent – illustrates the stranglehold the pharmaceutical industry and its associated players can have on consumers. Farma, Will Patrick's prototype bioreactor for the home, is a potential game-changer. It brews genetically modified algae to produce medicine, instantly turning humble kitchens into pharmacies. According to Patrick's concept, Farma owners will be able to order starter cultures for whatever drug they need and, eventually, have a daily supply of remedies for personal use. Thanks to the accompanying pill-maker, Farma's grow-it-yourself medicine should be much easier to swallow than anything the big-name corporations have to offer. — **WG**

iamwillpatrick.com

KETTAL

50 years of
outdoor furniture

FLORIM

MOOD

M

CONTEMPORARY PROJECT

Surfaces in a color project.
Casamood project finds its origin in color research. Color as necessity. Necessity to understand and define the place where you live, by creating and fulfill your mood, your own state of mind. With Neutra 6.0 floors and walls turn into emotional backgrounds as expressions of intimate desire.

casamood
MADE IN FLORIM

SPACEBALLS

Photos Lukas Renlund

Ikea sets out to explore the future of living

'What happens when a giant like Ikea takes on the design world?' The question was posed in *Frame* 105, in a feature that acknowledged such a giant's 'power to change things'. Remarkably, change is the order of the day at Space 10, an innovation lab the Swedish furniture company recently opened in Copenhagen to explore the future(s) of urban living. Every three months, an international community of creative thinkers led by Rebel Agency tackles a new theme that focuses on part of the home, including activities in the kitchen. For the lab's Tomorrow's Meatball project, chef Simon Perez and 'creative in residence' Bas van de Poel put a fresh spin on Ikea's signature dish, concocting eight meatballs, each based on a different sustainable food source. Contents ranged right down the food chain from algae and arachnid to locally grown ingredients and recycled edibles. — WG

space10.io

DANCE PARTNERS

Photos Todd Rosenberg

FRAM3 Waltz into Steven Holl's architectural wonderland with the digital magazine

Steven Holl's architecture inspires and invigorates Jessica Lang's choreography

Once you understand the creative process, you can apply it to anything, but the way in which that process is used to explore time and space varies widely. Dance performance *Tesseracts of Time* is the culmination of a research project, Explorations of IN, that architect Steven Holl and choreographer Jessica Lang spent a year and a half developing for the Chicago Architecture Biennial. Using the four seasons as a guide, they questioned how built form and dance – one static and long-lasting, the other temporary and continuously evolving – can push each other to generate a fascinating dialogue. During the four parts of the performance, dancers move under, in, on or over four types of architecture, with differing degrees of interaction. Space informs the use of time, physical finesse, dancers' reactions and moods conveyed. Holl and Lang's collaboration goes beyond previous attempts to unite architecture and choreography and fuels the search for further innovative alliances. — JM

stevenholl.com
jessicalangdance.com

Tom Dixon. INDUSTRIAL LANDSCAPE No 5 - BLUR

Inspired by the streets of London and the gritty backdrops of railways, tunnels of factories, workshops and warehouses. The surfaces – cracked paving stones and brick blocks make up the crumbling industrial landscape while the massive tidal River Thames splits the city in two, and the new reflective glass towers start to dominate the skyline.

The new Industrial Landscape collection is a series of seven carpet designs created by Tom Dixon in collaboration with ege carpets. Available in tiles and broadloom transforming into different expressions that reinterpret the rough, raw everyday surfaces that define the London landscape.

London – The Industrial Landscape. New carpet collection by Tom Dixon. **Learn more at egecarpets.com**

THE URGE TO EXPLORE SPACE

A digital animation makes a volatile image seem tactile

Signature, a short animation by Berlin-based outfit Colors And The Kids (CATK), offers an incredibly tactile impression despite its digital origins. Set against an electronic soundtrack and a peachy backdrop, a ropelike object comprising multicoloured, marbled and cracked segments slithers and slides midair, eventually assuming the shape of the studio's logo. CATK created the clip to symbolize its diverse nature and talent for mimicking texture – and aptly titled it *Signature*. — **EM**

c a t k . d e

Get mesmerized by CATK's *Signature* with the digital magazine

CURVE YOUR COLOURS

SHARP SHOOTERS

A bartending robot serves up a dose of big-data reality

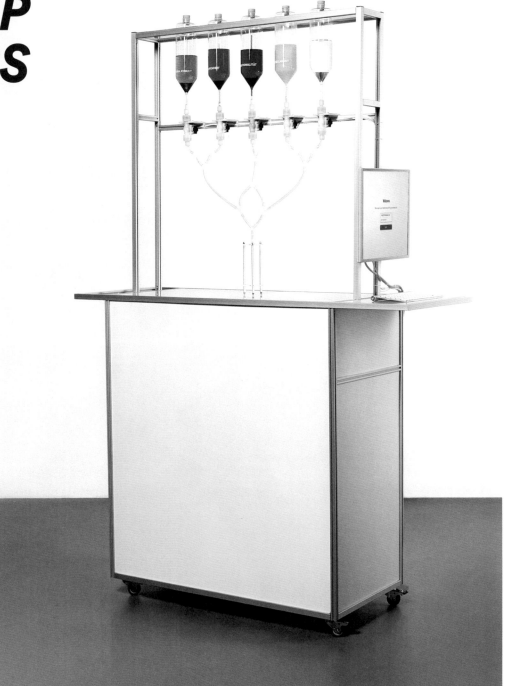

The fact that the internet devours and stores personal information is often the furthest thing from our minds as we surf the web. In order to visualize the impact of big data and the influence of algorithms on our daily lives, a group of students and graduates from Kunsthochschule Kassel devised The Social Shot, a mobile bartending robot. Using an algorithm developed at the University of Cambridge, the makers created a robot that analyses the personality traits of an individual based on information gleaned from their Facebook profile and serves up a representative layered cocktail. The aim of the project is to 'ironize the mass customization of nearly every imaginable product'. In doing so, the team behind The Social Shot draws attention to big data in a tasty 20-cl test tube. — **EM**

social-shot.com

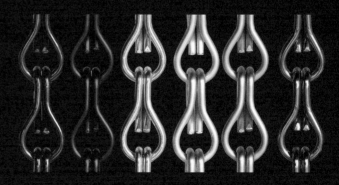

SENTIDO
THE LIGHT SWITCH REINVENTED

The Sentido switch equals **simplicity**, **comfort** and **quality**.

The whole surface is **touch-sensitive** and lights can be controlled at the slightest touch.

Sentido is designed to **work with KNX**, the international standard for home automation.

www.basalte.be | info@basalte.be

Fernando Laposse's tribute to corn highlights the destruction of local agriculture in Mexico

In response to the Mexican government's efforts to persuade farmers to cultivate genetically modified maize, Fernando Laposse constructed Totomoxtle, a pair of objects that celebrate the country's staple and extraordinarily diverse crop. The project comprises two pieces, which highlight the culinary and cultural richness of corn through the texture, colour and structure of the plant's husk.

One work combines thousands of laser-cut corn-husk fragments in an ornate tapestry of over 50 varieties of Mexican-grown grain. The other, which sees a cob of corn cradled in the grips of red-hot coloured tube lighting, expresses Laposse's experience of being taught to cook the grain by Mexican micro-business owners. Totomoxtle (the term means 'corn husks' in the Zapotec language) allows viewers to contemplate a way of life that's threatened by the hidden economic strain of corporate farming. — CW

fernandolaposse.com

KERNELS OF WISDOM

Subscribe Now

1 year of *Frame* for €99
+ free Muuto Grain lamp

Designed by Jens Fager, Grain is a versatile, environmentally friendly pendant lamp. The edge and hidden cord lock give Grain its character. Thanks to the lamp's matt surface, which is made from a special mix of bamboo grain and plastic composite, the product has a unique look and feel.

Height: 18.5 cm
Diameter: 21 cm

FREE
~~€119~~
Available only in black

FRAME	#108	JAN / FEB 2016	WORK ▏
FRAME	#107	NOV / DEC 2015	MATERIALS ▏▏▏▏▏▏
FRAME	#106	SEP / OCT 2015	HOSPITALITY ▏▏▏▏▏
FRAME	#105	JUL / AUG 2015	PRODUCTS ▏▏▏▏
FRAME	#104	MAY / JUN 2015	RETAIL ▏▏▏
FRAME	#103	MAR / APR 2015	COLOUR ▏▏

Includes free access to the digital version of the magazine

Limited stock available. Order today at
frameweb.com/subscribe-muuto

Offer is valid only until 30 April 2016

Ronan and Erwan Bouroullec tell their shared story. **Germaine Kruip** gives in to the dark side. **Snarkitecture** shows what shaped the studio. **Galila Barzilaï-Hollander** takes stock of her collection. **Ghaith&Jad** embraces Beirut's blemishes. **Eugeni Quitllet** talks life from *matin* to *noche*. All this and more perspectives on people.

Portraits

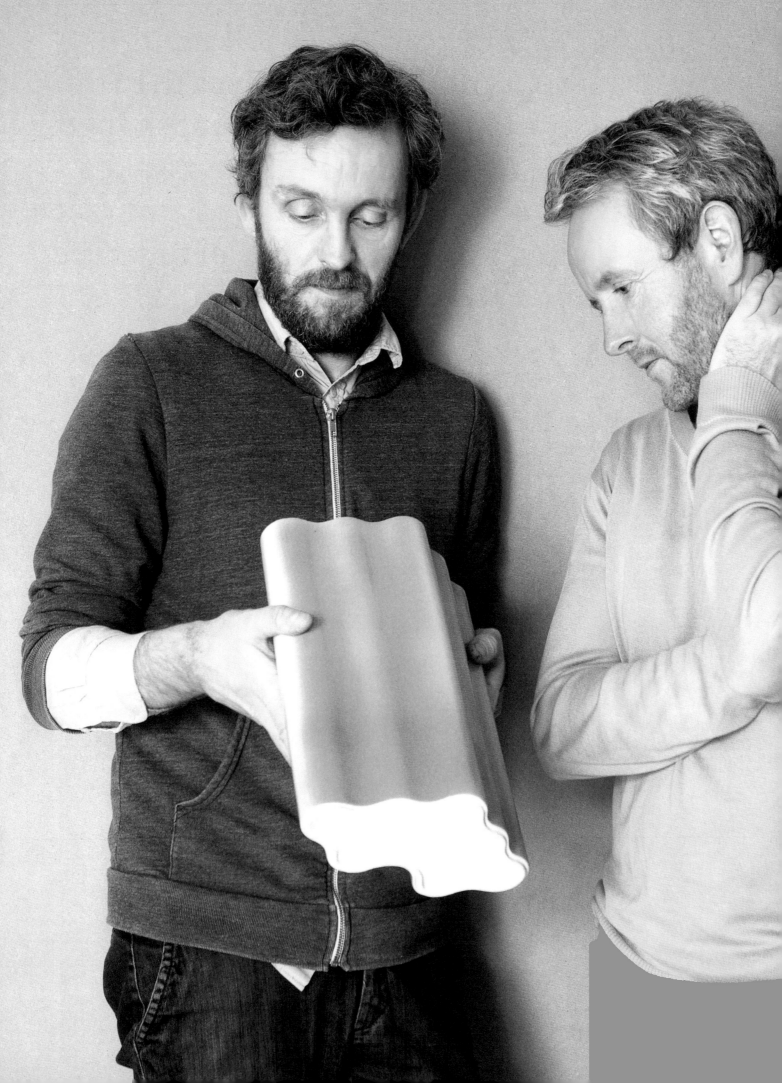

Four Hands Make Light Work

From learning to sew to discovering American design: the Bouroullec brothers reflect on the encounters and influences that shaped their collaborative careers.

WORDS *Melanie Mendelewitsch* **PORTRAITS** *Valentin Fougeray*

RONAN BOUROULLEC: 'Our grandparents were farmers from northern Finistère. DIY – home improvements and repairs – was part of their daily routine. Our parents weren't into manual labour, but they taught us a lot about things like making repairs and gardening. Ever since we were young, we've been tinkering away – it's something we taught ourselves to do.'

ERWAN BOUROULLEC: 'Ronan originally studied applied arts – first at Olivier de Serres [École Nationale Supérieure des Arts Appliqués et des Métiers d'Arts] and then at Ensad [École nationale supérieure des Arts Décoratifs]. Given our family background, it was easier to study design than to go to art school. It was a more recognized discipline, which had a clear purpose, while art was not as easy for some family members to understand. A few years later I went on to study fine arts at Cergy-Pontoise.'

'There are few women with whom we've developed products; engineers are most often men. When it comes to *textile*-related techniques, though, there are generally many female engineers, prototypers and so on. This echoes our family background: our father would look at a project from a structural perspective – he was doing heavy physical work with materials like wood and metal – whereas our mother taught us sewing and finer handicrafts. Women and men have a different approach to making, and I personally love the subtlety of the feminine way. It's linked with a better ability to concentrate.'

RB: 'Our four-handed approach began after we joined forces in 1999. Our relationship has evolved over the course of various projects. We've developed a greater maturity in our work. We've also managed to establish some sort of freedom. We used to confer and analyse our designs at every step of the way. Nowadays we work more independently, allowing things to grow before questioning ourselves.'

'We currently have a team of ten in our workshop. Erwan and I facilitate projects in much the same way as a conductor directs an orchestra. When one of us is hesitant about doing a project, that moment of doubt may lead to a more critical examination. Techniques and constraints are reassuring and form guidelines of sorts, but these are parameters that concern the maker rather than the user. Sometimes one of us is very much inside the project while the other maintains some distance, which allows him to see more clearly, because he doesn't get confused by the details.' ↳

↰EB: 'The real challenge of design is to learn how to distance oneself while maintaining control. The fact that we're a duo brings an almost schizophrenic dimension to our work.'

'We learned a lot from Giulio Cappellini. He's one of the first people who really listened to us and entrusted us with projects. I'm inspired by his intuition and by the way he's wrapped himself up in the Italian industry while maintaining a bold vision. He once told us that he never has bestsellers but *long*sellers. Many of his products weren't quick to sell but would find their "customer" later and establish themselves over a longer period. We've never forgotten this example.'

'Rolf Fehlbaum of Vitra also taught us a lot. In a way, you could compare him to a football coach; he helped us to improve and develop. When we started working together, he asked us to conceive office furniture, even though we'd never worked in a large office before. We were able to research an unfamiliar environment with an almost naive state of mind. As soon as we completed Joyn, our first product for Vitra, Rolf emphasized the need to maintain ingenuity. We continually try to follow his advice and keep a certain "unprofessionalism" and naivety in our practice. Everyone at our studio is young; it's often their first job.'

'Prototypers, technicians and engineers have taught me a lot – but you have to collaborate with them in a subtle way. Some of them can be reluctant to oppose our vision or to tell us what they *really* think. They can be closed off and hard to move. I recently understood the need to envision a part of our work as a harvest of knowledge, techniques and flavours. If we can't hear or broaden a technician's opinions, the "harvest" idea is lost. There are many ways to do this, but simple handmade prototypes and sketches often open up the discussion more than technical documents or 3D models can do.'

'It's impossible to work without an awareness of history. The older we get, the more we see design as a Darwinian phenomenon.'

'Because I studied fine arts, real design influences came to me later on. In a way, I have a polar view of design. I was impressed by the Americans, who had a joyful and positive way of addressing the largest audience through industrial production. Examples are Hans and Florence Knoll, George Nelson, Eero Saarinen and, of course, Charles and Ray Eames. Their work was typical of the American optimism of the '60s. Italian designers came later: Ettore Sottsass, Alessandro Mendini, Andrea Branzi and so on. Their punk approach was a real provocation against bourgeois common sense.'

RB: 'We're fascinated by the structure of vegetation. The organic – the logic and performance of the living – is so compelling. Plants often provide inspiration for structural research, although the results never try to mimic nature. But sometimes we seek some sort of opposition to constructed space – to the flat, orthogonal, monochromatic environment. We look for an almost animistic presence.'

EB: 'The French culture was not quite ready for the emergence of design as a practice. It remains very marked by the *mobilier de style*, and for many design is just another contemporary "style". French manufacturers and craftsmen have begun to understand the purpose of designers and to see designers as people who conceive products *with* and *for* them. We're facing quite a terrifying no-man's-land here. In places like Italy and the Nordic countries, however, design is inherently part of the culture.'

'The fundamental role of design is to give shape to culture. When you visit a museum devoted to ancient civilization, design – more specifically: the shape of everyday tools, weapons, jewellery and the like – is often the only thing that remains. Being able to stand the test of time means that those tools are technically perfect and were useful, but on top of that you see the people *behind* them. You see their humanity and can determine, therefore, the shape of their culture.'

'For many, design is

'The challenge is to re-establish a common understanding between manufacturers and users, as these two parties are becoming increasingly detached from each other.'

'Most of the companies we work with share a 1970s vision. It's home-oriented, based on sustainable domestic environments that barely change. When it comes to ecology, the idea of indestructible pieces of furniture that will last forever is essential. We don't want our objects to grow old or to be tied to a particular time period. The design of the '90s focused on screaming about deep change and a new aesthetic: a conception that gave birth to noisy objects that were too specific to age in harmony.'

'Alcove, a sofa for Vitra [2007], is one of our most successful projects, because it goes beyond the idea of a simple piece of furniture; it also organizes space. Alcove is the best summary of our Lit Clos [a sleeping cabin manufactured by Cappellini in 2000]; the concept is almost the same. But Lit Clos didn't sell at the time.'

'In our opinion, design can be shown in galleries, too. The gallery is an interesting place to remove oneself from the extremely rational framework of industrial production, to look for new paths or simply to express approaches that are too radical for large-scale production. Of course, since we're in a time of hyper velocity and the "starification" of designers, the legitimacy of the gallery can be questioned. In our case, though, we feel that the gallery is a necessary place to work – it goes hand in hand with the more traditional practice of product design.'

'For us, art feels like a surgical operation. Design, on the other hand, is akin to a form of homeopathy.' ✕
bouroullec.com

just another "style"

JSPR

SKETCH

WORDS *Ronald Hooft*
PORTRAIT *Raw Color*

OCCASIONALLY – feeling sentimental, often during a staff outing at the end of the year, with the dark days of Christmas time looming large, having savoured a hearty meal and, admittedly, mellowed by the demon drink – I succumb to the urge to tell my young colleagues and companions about the good old days. About a period that offered a meagre three options to those looking for ways to cover their floors. The average family chose wall-to-wall carpeting for the living room. Directly from the roll, with a width of 4 m and preferably in a repeat pattern, which showed the dirt less easily. If you were on a tight budget, you settled for lino. Easy to clean and, when skilfully installed, a smooth surface you could walk on for years, like a determined wife on her well-trained husband. It goes without saying that people in wealthier circles were partial to parquet. Polished once a year, mopped regularly – the proverbial piece of cake.

At this point I stop for a dramatic pause, which lengthens until someone can no longer bear the silence and breaks the tension with a muted cough or the audible scrape of a chair leg. Contemporary interior architects, designers and stylists consider it their job to guide demanding clients through the impenetrable jungle of flooring.

Floors made from hardwood originating in Asia, South America and darkest Africa, or from conifers grown in the United States, Scandinavia and Slavic regions. Timber sawed into broad planks and laid in a herringbone pattern, in Hungarian point, in Roman bond. Finely honed, unplaned, stained, whitewashed, varnished.

Reused planks from Canadian grain elevators destroyed in November storms, from demolished Trans-Siberian Railway coaches or even old school buildings. Planks composed of pulverized coconut husks or compressed bamboo shoots.

Natural stone from Pakistan, travertine from Izmir, bluestone from Belgium or Wales, marble from Cararra. Ceramic tiles that look like natural stone from Pakistan, like travertine from Izmir, like marble from – you get the picture. Speaking of ceramic: tile, which never really went out of style, is making a comeback.

Moroccan tiles, Spanish tiles, Portuguese tiles, often in combination with hardwood flooring from elsewhere in Europe.

Minimalists who want a good return for the investment made in underfloor heating often opt for a concrete floor. Sounds simple, but the opposite is true. Learning to finish concrete correctly means following an intensive six-month course. Only those diligent enough to pass with high marks can sum up the precise differences between steel-trowelled concrete, polished sand cement, micro concrete, egaline concrete, *béton ciré* and tadelakt – not to mention the various types of poured-resin floors.

If you're at wit's end by now and haven't a clue how to proceed, I suggest ordering wall-to-wall carpeting. Or maybe a nice smooth expanse of linoleum that's sure to last for years. ✕

Clothing courtesy of Ontour

Floors

Dutch architect and columnist Ronald Hooft reviews the past and present of flooring for the home.

Galila Barzilaï-Hollander believes her collection helps to explain aspects of who she is in a nonverbal way.

By the Book

Galila Barzilaï-Hollander may have stumbled into the world of art and design, but her growing collection is anything but accidental.

WORDS *Anne van der Zwaag* **PHOTOS** *Wouter Van Vaerenbergh*

I FIRST met Galila Barzilaï-Hollander about five years ago in Rotterdam. The occasion was Object, a contemporary design fair under my direction. She bought Richard Hutten's Book Chair, a purchase that didn't go unnoticed. Although the object *can* be used as a seat, it's much more a work of art than a functional piece of furniture – price-wise as well. Galila – who's referred to on a first-name basis in the business – has acquired numerous chairs, such as the vibrant Blue Rope Chair by Tom Price, which she bought from Belgian 'designart dealer' Victor Hunt. Today, Galila is a welcome guest at art and design fairs worldwide.

I don't have to travel far for our appointment. Her residence-cum-office is in Belgium, on a cul-de-sac amid rolling hills. A sign on the main façade – 'Tell me who I am' – is a prelude, welcoming visitors to a very personal universe. My first stop is the office, where I'm taken aback at the sight of a multitude of design and art pieces, many not yet unpacked. I immediately recognize work by Dutch studio Tjep., Belgian artist Christophe Coppens and British designer Tom Dixon.

Galila's passion for collecting contemporary art and design began in March 2005 during a trip to New York City. She and her husband, married for 30 years, had made a close-knit, hard-working team. The couple shared a passion for collecting antiquities. After her husband passed away in 2004, Galila decided to escape Europe and visit New York – a city where, as she says, 'one is never alone'.

She made the trip in March, which happens to be the month of The Armory Show, New York's international art fair. Her interest in antiques led Galila to presume the event was about armour. Following a few moments of hesitation – and realizing how ridiculously uninformed she was – she entered the unfamiliar territory and made her first purchase within 15 minutes. Unknowingly, Galila had landed in the heart of contemporary art, where she remains to this day. What's more, she's expanded that world to embrace contemporary design.

A sign by Jens Gussek on the façade of Barzilaï-Hollander's Belgian home – 'Tell me who I am' – welcomes guests to the collector's private world.

Known as 'the collector on the run', Galila flits from destination to destination: think Buenos Aires, Mexico, Stockholm, Milan, Vienna and London for starters. Her schedule includes an impressive series of annual fairs. 'Art and design were a sort of life-saver at the beginning. Now they are my oxygen.' Basel is a social must, she tells me. 'First of all, everyone is there, but I also go because of all the parallel fairs, where there are discoveries to make.' These smaller events are a means of encountering young and emerging talents – her main focus. ↳

↰ At first glance, Galila appears to have an outgoing personality and a wardrobe dedicated to clothing by Issey Miyake. Here at home, however, I find her leading a rather secluded life surrounded by her collection. Does she see these works as an extension of herself? Yes, the pieces she chooses help to explain aspects of who she is in a nonverbal way. The work of art at the door – 'Tell me who I am' – speaks volumes.

We have lunch at the house, which she's recently 'tidied up'. I remember my last visit here, when both house and office were crammed to the hilt, and 'crammed' is still an apt description. How many objects are we talking about? The answer is a smile. 'I feed many artists and designers from all over the world.'

Certain themes in the collection have caught my eye. I see what she calls 'money works', such as Dutch designer Rolf Bruggink's Penny Bench. The category incorporates a large group of objects linked to money, a subject that fascinates Galila, who holds a degree in psychology. 'All works relate to one another, and together they tell a story. Themes like eyes, paper, eggs and money were not something I planned; they simply happened.'

Are her acquisitions based purely on intuition, or does she have a shrewd strategy? When she started collecting, her lack of knowledge about contemporary art was an advantage. Her selections were not based on familiar names but on an intuitive feel for quality. This approach led to her purchase of work by Belgian designer Maarten De Ceulaer, as well as that of emerging Dutch designers Pepe Heykoop and Dirk Vander Kooij, still relatively fresh in collectors' circles. She relies on her business acumen and sense of fairness when considering prices. 'I never ask for a discount but for the best possible price.'

The words of a woman who's not really at home in the realm of design, but one with a keen eye. 'What I worship most in all aspects of life is creativity,' she says, 'and design is the result of a very creative approach and corresponding attitude. Designers make you see things differently.' The term she uses is *détournement*, while pointing out an example from her collection: a chair that functions as a radiator and vice versa. 'When we use the word "design", we're describing usable things, but some chairs can't be used and some art is

usable. I love the playfulness expressed in such work; it reveals a hidden part of me.'

She maintains close contact with a number of galleries but stays on the sideline. 'I don't belong to the galleries; the choices are mine.' Generally speaking, Galila avoids vernissages, calling them social events where the artist or designer in question is sometimes overlooked entirely. She values good relationships with artists and designers and says she's had only positive experiences with those she's met. From time to time, such affiliations lead to decidedly personal, often intimate commissions. At the moment, Tejo Remy is making a customized version of his famous Rag Chair out of clothes she's worn.

Galila has never sold a piece from her collection, because each is a cherished part of the family. Hers is the collection of someone who doesn't like the term 'collector', preferring to be called an 'artoholic' or an 'art-and-design addict'. According to Galila: 'The notion of danger makes the experience more exciting.' ✕

Galila poses alongside Tejo Remy's Chest of Drawers, a criticism on consumerism that can also be found in the collections of museums such as MoMA.

Barzilaï-Hollander is drawn to playful pieces, such as objects that seem usable but aren't – and vice versa. Bruno Munari's *Bottiglia Lampo (Hommage à Marcel Duchamp)* is a glass bottle with a zipper.

Money – a category that includes works such as Dutch designer Rolf Bruggink's Penny Bench – is a recurring theme in Galila's collection.

'Themes like eyes, paper, eggs and money were not something I planned; they simply happened'

Eugeni Quitllet oscillates between the pace of Paris and the peace of Barcelona to balance daily life.

WORDS *Will Georgi* PORTRAIT *Anna Huix*

Heigh-Ho,

EUGENI QUITLLET: Where do I live? Good question. At the moment I'm split between Barcelona and Paris, but Barcelona is home – and where my office is. Wherever I am in the world, I wake up and go to bed at the same time if I don't have jet lag: 7:30 in the morning, 10:30 at night. It's not a matter of mental or physical discipline. I simply need to sleep well, and I like going to sleep early. If it's Sunday, I might sleep in until 9.30 a.m., but I like daytime and the morning light – it's fresh and optimistic. There's a seasonal difference, though: part of the year when the sun is already out in Barcelona, it's still dark in Paris.

Normally I go out to have breakfast. When I get home, I've changed my mind-set and feel as if I'm arriving at the office. I live and work in Barcelona with my wife and our five-year-old daughter, who really inspires me. She loves to play and draw, and when she draws, she's got this thing at the moment where she'll say: 'Don't interrupt. I'm working.' I thought of her when I made the tableware toy for Air France. Children were the client's priority – and mine as well – because when a child is relaxed in the air, the flight is much better for everyone.

I like to mix family and work whenever possible. If speed isn't of the essence, our kitchen is open, and people can drop in for a drink. In order to find ideas, we should be open to what's happening around us. If all we do is concentrate, we miss out on a lot. One of my problems is a failure to distinguish between different activities. For me, a vacation is another place to work, but in a different way. Last summer I flew to California and met a guy in Santa Barbara: Neal Feay makes the most beautiful aluminium on the planet. I'm about to go back again, with the family, to work a little bit and have fun.

When I'm in Paris, I'll grab a salad or sandwich for lunch and go back to work straightaway. In Barcelona, people go home to eat lunch, which lasts at least an hour and a half. I feel free in both cities, but they have different energies. After the speed of Paris it's good to come back to a quiet place with nice light, where I can slow down and work freely.

Every idea still begins with pen and paper, but the quality isn't the same as it was when I had no computer and made beautiful drawings. Now I just do a sketch so I won't forget what I want to explain to my colleagues.

I don't make models, and I don't like having lots of pieces of paper around that *could* be something but are still nothing. I like things to be finished in my brain before we start to design; only then do I shape directly inside the virtual space of my computer. It would be perfect if I could link my brain to a 3D printer; it would save a lot of time.

Design is good, because it allows you to invent and reinvent your everyday life to make something new; nothing is here to stay. For me, design is an optimistic way to see the future: it's a feeling of positivity into which you project your

dreams and ideas about what you want to do. All beautiful things are in the future. When you're depressed, you revisit the past.

I finish work by 8 p.m. at the latest. We don't like to keep working until deep in the night. We eat at home if we have our daughter with us; otherwise, we meet friends and go out for a meal. How do I relax? I sleep. I like to go driving. At the weekend I sometimes head to the sea, which is just an hour's drive away. I relax when I work, too. I listen to music – a lot of electronic music and radio from Ibiza, like OpenLab – and go with the flow. I grew up in Ibiza, and electronic music was the only popular music we had. It wasn't anything sophisticated, just natural.

I'd like to be able to read when I go to bed, but I fall flat after two pages. I like to read fiction, but I always envision the action, which makes it feel as if I'm reading somebody else's film. I love to dream. I dream all day long – not just about other products, but also about other realities and other worlds. So when I read, I choose something really fantastic or get into a real-life story or philosophy – something I can learn from. ✕

At Salone del Mobile in April, Eugeni Quitllet will present the world's most expensive toilet brush, which he designed for Pomd'or. 'What makes it expensive? Everything, from the way it's done to the material. It's very minimal. I'd like to do something cheaper, but this is a beautiful paradoxical object.'
eugeniquitllet.com

Heigh-Ho

Eugeni Quitllet's lightweight Wall Street chair for Vondom is as suitable for the seaside as for the city – a notion that's fitting for a designer who divides his time between Barcelona and Paris.

soft collection by molo

The Dark Side

Relying heavily on the power of shadows, Germaine Kruip creates voids for her audience to fill.

WORDS *Jane Szita* PORTRAITS *Anne Claire de Breij*

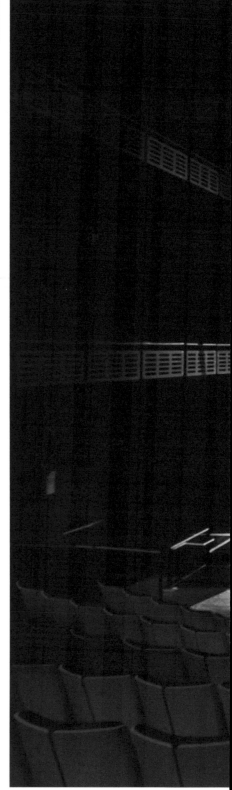

Photo Kris Qua

DUTCH artist Germaine Kruip began her career in the theatre after studying scenography. Later, a residency at the Rijksakademie in Amsterdam kick-started her work as a visual artist. Her pieces – from mechanized sculptures to collaborations with Raf Simons for Jil Sander stores – invite audience involvement through their unresolved ambiguity, an effect often achieved with shadows. Kruip lives and works in Amsterdam and Brussels.

How did you start working with shadows?
GERMAINE KRUIP: *Counter Shadow* was the first piece I made that explored the subject. In the work, a sculpture casts a shadow that is fixed like a stage prop, in contrast with a moving light. Like *Counter Composition*, a kinetic piece I made afterwards, the object is deconstructed into light and shadow. The shadow presents itself like the ghost of a work. It's like a meditation on appearing and disappearing, or a search for a moment

between the two. A shadow is a void, and that's not entertaining or pleasing; for some, including me, it's vaguely threatening. Shadows always represent something else; they trigger the imagination.

Why did you make the switch from theatre to art? The question was: *Why do I have to imitate life in the theatre, when life is already so theatrical?* Instead of adding things, like you do as a scenographer, I wanted to subtract – to arrive at another view. My art is a kind of reverse process. At Art Basel, for instance, I made a reverse spotlight using a gobo [a lighting stencil]. I made a point of *shadow*, not light, on the floor – like an absent person. It's about creating an emptiness that the audience can fill with expectation.

In your current exhibition at the Oude Kerk in Amsterdam, one work involves removing *all* the lights. *Oude Kerk Untitled* involves a kind of negative art direction. Taking all ↳

'I create an emptiness

In 2014 *A Possibility of an Abstraction* appeared at the Experimental Media and Performing Arts Center in Troy, New York. During the performance, which will be part of Kunstenfestivaldesarts in Brussels this May, a large shadow emerges from an empty stage.

that the audience can

Photos Gert Jan Kocken

The Wavering Skies saw an ominous shifting cloud loom over the entrance passage of London's Frieze Art Fair in 2005.

↰the lights away from the church allows the shadows to return, and they are constantly changing. When I begin any installation, I always start by removing everything, including the light sources.

Is there an element of confrontation in your work? Sometimes. For Frieze Art Fair I did a piece called *The Wavering Skies* in which a dark cloud moves over the entrance hall. Art fairs are constantly bright, like a casino. I wanted to add a different, slightly alarming, reality.

Your work calls for active observation. That's why the titles don't have a message – I am not telling people what to see. In *Simultaneous Contrast*, it's about a mental shadow, a kind of optical illusion. Two half circles move very fast, and you start to see a dark shadow spot. It's done with very detailed programming – very technical – but the whole point is to highlight the process that occurs in the gap between the eye and the brain.

How do people react to your pieces? They get involved. They sometimes ask: *Why is this art?* I don't consider that a negative remark at all. Art is about questioning things, not providing answers. Anyone is qualified to look at art. I don't make a distinction between art critics and tourists. I believe in the public.

Theatre seems to be returning to your work. After 15 years as a visual artist, I do have one foot back in the theatre. In May I'm showing *A Possibility of an Abstraction* at Kunstenfestivaldesarts in Brussels. People sit around an empty stage as a big black shadow – a void – appears. They then see a diamond floating and changing shape. They have to actively *look*; in fact, they end up on the edge of their seats. I worked with a theatrical team and we had rehearsals, but there are no actors. It's about the collective gaze – the audience creates the work by looking. ✕

Germaine Kruip: Geometry of the Scattering is on show at the Oude Kerk in Amsterdam until 27 March 2016
germainekruip.com

fill with expectation'

ZEITRAUM

ALS EIGENSTÄNDIGES
EINZELMÖBEL HÄLT
KIN BIG AUCH FÜR
UNKONVENTIONELLE
ANWENDUNGEN
LÖSUNGEN BEREIT UND
BIETET EFFIZIENTE
VERSTAUUNGSMÖGLICHKEITEN.

AS A
STAND-ALONE
PIECE OF FURNITURE,
KIN BIG OFFERS
EFFICIENT
STORAGE SOLUTIONS
FOR A WIDE
RANGE OF TASKS.

KIN – STORAGE SYSTEM
DESIGN BY
MATHIAS HAHN, 2016

zeitraum-moebel.de

Scar
Tissue

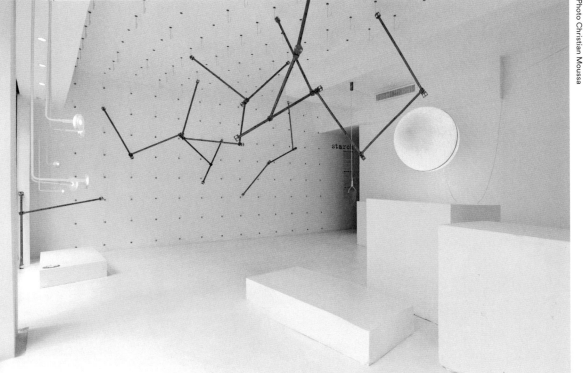

Photo Christian Moussa

Working with Beirut's blemishes, Ghaith&Jad injects sensitive architecture into a historically rich city.

WORDS *Shonquis Moreno* **PORTRAITS** *Joe Kesrouani*

Ghaith Abi Ghanem (left) and Jad Melki pose alongside one of their experiments with light, form and texture. Their boutique for Starch Foundation (above) is an adaptable installation that translates the organization's constantly changing line-up of creatives.

IN FEW places on earth are destruction and creation, sophistication and nihilism, bound in such a tangled embrace as in Beirut: glamorous Beirut, of the sun-drenched Corniche, was called the Paris of the Middle East even after wrenching its independence from France in 1943. By 1975, however, the Lebanese Civil War had cut the city in two, making Beiruti architecture a tortured body of regional politics and turning it into a wasteland of bullet-pocked façades, violently exposed concrete reinforcement and rubble.

Into this devastation enter architects Jad Melki (1988) and Ghaith Abi Ghanem (1990), who were born as the war was fading into a fraught peace. Tucked into their studies at the American University of Beirut was an internship at the Basel offices of Swiss architects Jacques Herzog and Pierre de Meuron. Along with that stint, subsequent awards for both young men encouraged them, following graduation in 2012, to join forces. They refurbished a tiled studio in a 1930s villa called Mansion, one of the city's few cultural co-working spaces, where light filters in through foliage and tall windows. Their projects – ranging from the Starch Foundation boutique and the Blue lamp series to the Brilliant Beirut exhibition design and an alpine residence that's still in the making – privilege process over aesthetic, collaboration over authorship and, instead of narrow specialization, the blurring of scales and disciplines.

Why did you open your office in Beirut?
GHAITH ABI GHANEM: Beirut is extremely rich in its historical formation and organic growth, from the days of the French Mandate until the end of the civil war. It holds many narratives and textures, as well as spatial layering in an urban and architectural sense, all of which enrich any design process, at any scale.

JAD MELKI: Beirut's rawness is a source of inspiration that feeds into our design process. And at Mansion, many ↳

To complement the graphic style of Rana Salam, who curated the Brilliant Beirut exhibition, Ghaith&Jad created a system of illuminated triangular volumes that united the diverse design materials on display.

↰multidisciplinary designers work under one roof. Within this space, we continue to explore emerging dialogues with the city.

How does the city's history of extremes between architectural annihilation and creativity affect your work?
GG: We grew up experiencing the rebirth of Beirut at a time of intense post-war reconstruction, so we witnessed various approaches to urban development. Some architects and developers reacted to an increased demand for housing and the urgent need for residential and commercial buildings, which changed the reading of the city from what it used to be before the war. In parallel, others wanted to turn architecture into an identical reconstruction of the old fabric, demolishing existing ruins and building exact replicas of old Beirut. In contrast, however, a few architects adopted a more sensitive policy, working with the city's scarred fabric and surgically adding responsive contemporary architecture to the urban environment.

JM: We are inspired by this method. As architects we prefer a more conceptual approach to building, where we read the context of a project through both its history and the way it is experienced now. Opening a studio at Mansion complements our way of thinking, because artists and designers here are working together to restore a dynamic spirit to other spaces just like it.

Where do you think the design and architecture industries are headed in Lebanon? GG: We see the design industry booming – especially product design. The architecture industry is also progressing, thanks to inspiring local architects like Youssef Tohme, Bernard Khoury and Raëd Abillama, as well as to international architects like Steven Holl, Zaha Hadid and Herzog & de Meuron. The latter are building here but, for various reasons, at a relatively slow pace. Politicized building laws and the high price of real estate are not conducive to responsive architecture. As a result, the majority of Lebanese projects are more commercial and profit-orientated.

How does your practice fit into that direction? JM: Having worked locally and abroad, we believe that design is largely a process of creation and not just the making of physical form. This process not only involves fabrication techniques and material investigation, but also questions accepted ideas and concepts. Our experimentation with basic elements – from raw building materials to everyday human experiences – generates a consistent line of thought that guides the design process and gives us an objective. By tackling these elements, we develop a project that's responsive to its site and that highlights its social and spatial qualities.

GG: Although we operate on different scales and work with briefs that range from architecture to product design, we avoid differentiation. Blurring and fusing the lines between categories of design is essential to our studio: it makes process *the* tool of creation. Once we achieve the level of freedom needed for exploration, we can push the boundaries of established design methodologies and come up with an alternative way to deal with any brief. ✕
ghaithjad.com

Using fluid materials like resin and freshly mixed concrete, Ghanem and Melki immortalize the moment when liquid clashes with water in their Blue series, a collection of objects that began with a lamp. The function of each one-off product is determined by this sudden confrontation.

'Blurring and fusing the lines between categories of design is essential to our studio'

Mark
This
Day

FREE BOOK

Photo Ola Studio

Bright 2

ARCHITECTURAL ILLUMINATION
AND LIGHT INSTALLATIONS

Artist Daniel Arsham and architect Alex Mustonen unearth five key moments in the Snarkitecture story.

WORDS *Shonquis Moreno*
PORTRAIT *Kyoko Hamada*

Going Solid

2011

Dig – a performance-cum-exhibition in New York City – set Snarkitecture on the path to experimentation in subtractive construction.

DIG, NEW YORK CITY

Brooklyn-based Snarkitecture – artist Daniel Arsham and architect Alex Mustonen, who devise everything from retail spaces, furniture and residential designs to lighting, art and stage sets – has always been a practice that is practised in excavation. It's as if the two are constantly digging for something essential and, once the unearthing is done, finding – like the mapless hunt for their namesake, Snark – that they have synchronously arrived at nothing and everything.

Project Dig was both performance and an intimate, thrilling exhibition through which to crawl. The work saw Arsham and friends use hammers, picks and chisels to carve a cavern from a room-size block of EPS architectural foam, which filled Steven Holl's richly seamed Storefront for Art and Architecture to bursting.

'Dig was formative in that we were finding the ground in which we wanted to experiment,' says Mustonen. While architecture is usually an additive process, they found their passion for subtractive construction in Dig. And the powerful reactions from the people exploring it spurred the Snarkitects to begin operating in the semi-public sphere, designing and realizing projects that engage wider audiences.

The digging of Dig was laborious, Arsham recalls with a wry grin, 'because I was the one over there excavating the damn thing. One thing we learned is that we don't always have to make everything ourselves. We hadn't configured the studio yet, so it was all hands on deck.' Mustonen is quick to jump in: 'It was very fluid.' Arsham clarifies with the words: 'And by fluid, he means chaotic.'

'We learned that we don't always have to make everything ourselves'

The entrance pavilion for Design Miami 2012, Drift was a lesson in reduction that informed future projects by Snarkitecture, such as The Beach.

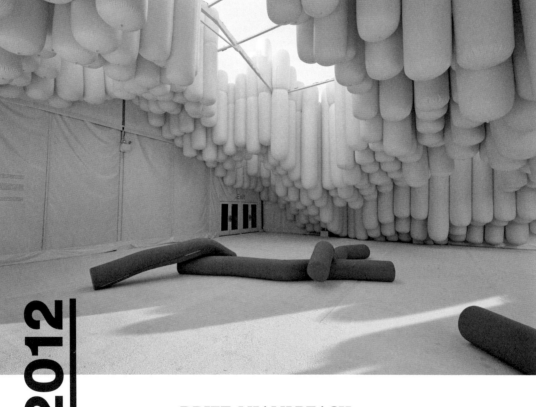

2012

Photo Markus Haugg

DRIFT, MIAMI BEACH

Arsham and Mustonen like to sabotage existing architecture, manipulate its structure, drag materials out of context, and ask you to *think* twice after making you *look* twice. In 2012 they achieved every one of these objectives in their plan for the Design Miami entrance pavilion. Drift turned a conventional white vinyl tent into a hanging garden of inflated white cylinders. The chubby tubes were visible from the street at a distance, while chinks between them filtered light and views of the sky to the delight of visitors inside. Arranged cheek by jowl, the objects conveyed a massive lightness, like architectural marshmallows or a cathedral of

featherweight punching bags. They hovered at different heights, leaving room for circulation paths below. Despite the singularly powerful-yet-ploofy look, the emphasis was not on the aesthetic. The design was a meditation on reduction, paring down to a single form, repeated on a vast scale, made of only one material (an approach that would later inform projects like The Beach). 'How can we reimagine architecture and ask people to reconsider it?' Mustonen asks, describing the goal of much of their work today. 'Drift set a very high standard for us in terms of what people think of our work,' says Arsham. 'It's still one of our most referenced projects when we talk to new clients.' ↳

A Memorial Bowing marked the expansion
of Snarkitecture's professional network. The
team called on a structural engineer and
lighting designers to assist with the project.

Photos Noah Kalina

2012

2015

A MEMORIAL BOWING, MIAMI

↰ In Arsham's early large-scale ink drawings, a
heavy geometric volume invades a pastoral scene
in which nature devours the ruins of something
anciently man-made. Scenes of meditation and
mortality – brand-newness asserted in a meadow
of melancholy wreckage – the drawings have
a surrealism that the studio revisits regularly.
Likewise, A Memorial Bowing reframes the
destruction of a 20th-century stadium and a
massive sign that advertised it for 71 years. The
studio dispersed the sign's 3-m-high 3D letters
over the east plaza of Marlins Park, filtering
views of the new baseball stadium through
memes of the old. The postures of the letters –
some stand tall, others have toppled over – serve
alternately as markers of ruin and rebuilding.

At this point the studio started to work
with specialists – a structural engineer and
lighting designers – who augmented the men's
skill and knowledge sets. Meanwhile the
budget, as well as the logistical complexity
and the distance between New York and
Miami, meant tighter structuring of studio
operations. A complicated relationship with
the client involved both county authorities
and the Marlins baseball team, the latter
of which 'didn't have a say', according to
Arsham, 'but did have an opinion'. It was
their first use of 'bold, intense' colour, their
first permanent piece and their first run-in
with city building codes. 'We had to negotiate
the exact position of each letter and follow
the same permission process as if we were
constructing a building,' Mustonen recalls.
'We were putting massive concrete lettering
in precarious positions. Sometimes I'm
surprised they let us do it.'

BEACH, WASHINGTON D.C.

In 2010 Arsham and Mustonen made scenography for modern dancers who improvised their movements around 10,000 ordinary white ping-pong balls that cascaded from the ceiling to bounce and roll randomly across the stage. More recently, the two choreographed an all-white architectural installation that abstracted a seashore under the gargantuan gilded Corinthian columns of the National Building Museum's Great Hall.

Using ordinary construction materials like scaffolding, drywall and mirrors, they undammed a sea of 750,000 recyclable plastic spheres to produce a recreational experience that resembled a ball pit for adults. 'This project had been floating around the studio for years in terms of the material and the idea of using a single-colour sphere. We wanted to flatten it out into a uniform tonality and create an environment with it,' says Arsham. The client for the largest project the studio had worked on to date was, ironically, a building museum also unversed in constructions of this scale. The not-for-profit organization helped the designers to build on a tight budget, however, by pulling in favours from board members (contractors), who donated labour to lower costs. Although designed for 40,000 visitors, The Beach accommodated almost five times that number. 'It broke the museum's record for attendance and took a lot of wear,' says Arsham. 'People around the world reached out to us about bringing the project to their locations.' This year, therefore, a 'new and improved version' of The Beach will go on tour. 'We can build on what we learned. It's a challenge to construct something that can travel to different venues.' ↳

At the time of writing, The Beach (2015) is Snarkitecture's largest project. When it goes on tour in 2016, the studio's work will move even further into the public spotlight.

'The Kith projects have broadened our reach in retail'

For their second Kith commission, a store in Brooklyn, New York, Snarkitecture was given a blank slate on which to explore new materials.

Photo Nolan Parsons

2015

KITH, BROOKLYN

↰ A decade ago, fashion designer Hedi Slimane hired Arsham to insert surreal works of art into existing Dior shops, warping the walls to look like drapery or tying two walls together in a bow. Snarkitecture's Kith clothing stores are not art, but design that feels artistic. The studio has evolved to allow Mustonen and Arsham to make art, design and/or a synthesis of the two. Presumably, this is why the artist teamed up with the architect: each, by complementing the other, unlocks a greater creative range that embraces their collective talents.

For their second Kith commission, they designed *everything* in the space. They were given a 'blank slate' on which to explore new materials while fashioning a distinct brand experience or, as it turned out, multiple experiences: a cereal and ice-cream bar with the subway-tiled spirit of an old-school automat, an exhibition space, and a ceiling installation of 700 white cast-replica Jordan II sneakers suspended above a white Carrara marble floor with a herringbone motif. The job demanded the help of various subcontractors – for millwork, flooring and lighting – a team of experts with whom Snarkitecture has built relationships based on high standards. 'Our fabricators have come to know what we expect of them,' says Mustonen. 'We scream at them less, but they understand that we won't sacrifice quality to save time or money.'

Two additional projects for the client are already in the works. 'The Kith projects have broadened our reach in retail,' says Arsham, 'but we've been so busy with them that we haven't had time to work with other brands.' ✕

snarkitecture.com

marset

Taking care of light

www.marset.com

<u>Adjaye Associates</u> covers all angles. **<u>Neri&Hu</u>** performs plastic surgery. **<u>March Studio</u>** channels post-war suburbia. **<u>Moment</u>** pulls passers-by into <u>Me Issey Miyake</u>'s web. <u>El Equipo Creativo</u> trawls the ocean for inspiration. It's the pick of the crop from the worlds of art and design.

Har vest

Photos Alan Tansey

softlabnyc.com

Get Back to Work

It's all eyes on SOFTlab's installation at Bēhance's New York City office

NEW YORK CITY — SOFTlab's construction methods may have moved beyond the humble paper clip, but the outfit's ability to transform spaces with a minimum of materials lives on. Asked by Bēhance to design an installation for its New York City office, the studio responded by linking the two-storey space with a sculpture visible from all corners of the workplace. The central stairwell that connects the levels was seen as the perfect spot to host the friendly parasite.

'The design of the office is very clean, with a lot of white finishes, so we decided to create an installation that acts as a kind of three-dimensional stained-glass window,

casting coloured light throughout the space,' says SOFTlab's Michael Szivos. The palette pulls shades from the visual identities of Bēhance and Adobe (Bēhance's parent company). 'We algorithmically generated a transition from red on one side of the stairwell to blue on the other,' says Szivos, 'and added a random mix of secondary colours to make the piece more vibrant.' The installation – made from a laser-cut Mylar net clad in laser-cut photo gels of different colours – also acts as a frame, drawing attention to a circular luminaire at its peak and communal seating at its base. — TI
softlabnyc.com

Photo Amedeo Benestante, courtesy of Madre Museum

NAPLES — Daniel Buren has a way of mixing up space and turning it inside out to weave new dimensions around exhibition visitors. While most often recognized for the signature 8.7-cm-wide stripes he's been painting since the 1960s, the French artist has developed an increasingly complex language over recent decades. *Axer / Désaxer*, Buren's site-specific installation showing at Madre Museum in Naples, is a prime example of the direction he's following.

Visitors enter an iridescent environment marked by the main motifs of the artist's aesthetic: black and white bands, wall-wide mirrors that multiply the volume of the room, and brightly coloured shapes positioned to highlight the building's architectural features. The piece not only establishes a relationship with the interior, but also produces an axial alliance between the museum and the street outside by altering depth and perspective in pure Buren fashion. Merely stepping over the threshold plays tricks with your perception, which becomes the centre of the work.

Curated by Andrea Viliani and Eugenio Viola to coincide with Madre's tenth anniversary, *Axer / Désaxer* is the second Buren to grace the institution's premises this year. The artist's earlier offering – a scaled-up 'kindergarten' made from geometric shapes – appeared alongside the installation until the end of February. — NB

Axer / Désaxer is on show at Madre Museum in Naples through 4 July 2016
danielburen.com

FRAM∃   Step into Daniel Buren's multiple dimensions with the digital magazine

Matter of Perspective

A site-specific work by Daniel Buren highlights the artist's increasingly complex language

Photos Lesha Yanchenkov

On the wall menu:

САЛАТЫ
руккола + годжи 50
кунжут + морковь
овощи + песто

ДЕСЕРТЫ
йогурт + гранола 40
желе + сливки
конфеты 15

НАПИТКИ
ваниль + лимонад 30
молоко + галка 25
кэроб + банан
имбирь + лимон 30
чай латте + специи 30
черный кофе 20
свежий сок 40
глинтвейн 40

KIEV — If you think of an orang-utan, chances are that white won't be the first colour to spring to mind – unless you conjure up a rather elderly creature. Yet that's exactly the colour that AKZ chose as the basis for restaurant Orang+Utan in Kiev, Ukraine.

Almost the entire interior is covered in standard white tiles; the only colour permitted to creep in comes via the food served, flashes of greenery in the bathroom and the odd piece of decorative fruit. The reason for AKZ's ultra-neutral palette is explored elsewhere in this issue (research into a potential link between colour and wellness begins on page 141), but if the right colour can boost health, you could

be forgiven for asking: *Why white?* The answer lies in the food. Orang+Utan is a vegetarian restaurant and all its sandwiches, smoothies and salads are, as the tiles convey, as unrefined as the driven snow.

Healthy food isn't all the ceramic material symbolizes, though. According to architects Artem Vakhrin and Katya Zuieva, white tiling has a deeper resonance for Kiev's older residents. In the days of the USSR, it appeared in every building, from hospitals to swimming pools. At that time, white tiles were the only kind available. Their presence in modern, independent Ukraine (in a vegetarian restaurant, *nota bene*) is a poignant reminder of how times change. — WG

akz-architectura.com

Monkey Business

A restaurant in Ukraine apes the past to serve up a taste of freedom

Photo Guillaume Ziccarelli, courtesy of the Aïshti Foundation

The Art of Shopping

Adjaye Associates covers all angles for a mall-cum-art gallery in Lebanon

BEIRUT — As heavyweights like Rem Koolhaas have long pointed out, art and shopping now have an almost wholly intertwined relationship. Arguably, nowhere is this liaison more obvious than at the Aïshti Foundation in Beirut, which was designed by Adjaye Associates. The new building is a pet project of Aïshti founder Tony Salamé. Located on a brownfield coastal site that is part of the city, the luxurious Lebanese complex brings together contemporary art and shopping enjoyment under a single roof.

Retail is positioned to one (curiously windowless) side of the seven-storey building, where outlets are clustered around a central atrium that draws in natural light. The 18,000-m^2 interior mixes mirror-clad and exposed-concrete columns with an anodized-aluminium mesh ceiling and a marble-patterned floor. Defining the east façade is a single large window, behind which a staircase leads to the 4,500-m^2 gallery space.

Overall flexibility was an important consideration. Although mall and gallery have separate entrances, everything is interconnected. The architect describes the building as a 'glazed box that sits within a louvred frame'. The outer layer is notable for its zigzagging pattern of red aluminium tubes, a motif that also appears on tiling inside the building. At the time of writing, the project awaits additional interior detailing, as well as the completion of a seaside promenade. — GG
adjaye.com

In the Cloud

Arboit Limited lends form to digital communication for a Chinese tech company

GUANGZHOU — We once thought of the internet as something invisible and used 'the virtual' to describe it. The data centres that make it possible for all those bytes to flow properly, however, are very real places that are generally characterized by a sober, industrial look. To brighten things up – and to make the company's architecture live up to the dynamic nature of the information it houses – Chinese internet-service outfit Cloud DCS asked Italian architect Alberto Puchetti and his Hong Kong-based firm Arboit Limited to plan and realize its Guangzhou headquarters. The ultimate goal was the creation of an iconic brand identity that would stand out 'in a competitive Chinese IT market that has generally shown no interest in design'.

The building is at the centre of the Pearl River Delta, a fast-growing tech hub that borders the South China Sea. The interior of the nearly 2,000-m^2 headquarters has a twofold nature: server rooms filled with buzzing machines and cooling pipes painted in different colours share the space with more human-orientated areas for staff and ↳

↰visitors. The latter are bathed in white and seven shades of blue, Cloud DCS's signature palette. A sleek, celestial atmosphere permeates lobby, offices, and meeting and control rooms.

The centrepiece of Arboit Limited's concept – streaming clouds, a vital part of the client's corporate identity – is a 1,050-m² showroom featuring various multimedia installations that highlight the services offered by Cloud DCS. On display are technical gadgets, accessories, 3D video screens made from plastic balls, interactive videos and more. Throughout the space, curves and reflective surfaces bearing images of clouds printed on resin or plastic film provide warmth and depth. Complementing prints on the floor is a layered ceiling-mounted sculpture that extends a full 30 m. It consists of fabric-covered metal profiles that symbolize digital communication across the globe.

The overall idea was to turn the impersonality of a typical IT workplace into a more pleasant environment and to imbue a Chinese workplace with a dash of American flair. Tables holding architectural models of future industrial parks proposed for the area suggest that Arboit and Cloud DCS intend to continue their collaboration. — NB
arboit.com

Photos Dennis Lo

Hong Kong studio Arboit Limited opted for
a brand-driven space to help Cloud DCS stand
out in the competitive Chinese IT market.

MELBOURNE — With a string of restaurants across the city, Jimmy Grants is one of Melbourne's most popular Greek souvlaki joints. In the past, the likes of Technē Architecture paved Jimmy's *food*steps with fit-outs focused on a theme unique to each outpost. The latest edition sees March Studio conjure the quintessential Australian post-war suburban brick house – a homage to Jimmy's private life.

Incorporating recycled cream brick and vintage wallpaper, the interiors evoke home-building techniques from 'back in the day', says March Studio's Rodney Eggleston. 'We took artist Howard Arkley's airbrushed suburban houses as a model.' As part of their research, Eggleston and team made a photography tour of Melbourne's Sunshine suburb, capturing 'brick arches and the raw-iron language of curved front fences and signs. We wanted to tap into some of those lost and forgotten art forms and trades.'

March's translation includes sweeping arches, brass fittings, rounded joinery and cheeky decor. The designers deliberately made the large site feel smaller and more intimate, an atmosphere that's accentuated by generous lighting that glistens off mirrors to bathe the space in a warm glow. As Eggleston says: 'The look and feel really points to that idea of home.' — AB
marchstudio.com.au

Home Cooking

Post-war suburbia is the unlikely inspiration for March Studio's design of the latest Jimmy Grants

Photos Peter Bennetts

Screen Play

Erwan
and Ronan
Bouroullec
play with
proverbial
fire and ice
in France

RENNES — 'In a way, we could compare
design to cooking. The challenge is to get
the most out of pre-existing flavours, to
reveal them. Those flavours are often found
in materials and techniques,' says Erwan
Bouroullec from the studio he shares with
his brother in Paris, just a stone's throw away
from the location of recent attacks on the
city. 'Our approach to 17 Screens was quite
similar: it's a quest for sensations stemming
from the deliberately extreme mix of
materials such as glass, ceramic, textile and
aluminium. What we tried to emphasize is the
elasticity between materials, between things
that don't necessarily fit together.'

After a stop at the Tel Aviv Museum
of Art, 17 Screens was transported to Rennes,
Brittany, the region that Erwan and Ronan
Bouroullec call home. The installation is part
of a vast threefold exhibition in which three
venues – Frac Bretagne, Les Champs Libres
and the Parliament of Bretagne – are uniting
to celebrate *les enfants du pays*.

The modular wall systems featured
in 17 Screens form a meandering path, a sort
of urban dreamscape whose composition
suggests the abstracted geometry produced
by a prism. Individual partitions seem to
meld together in a fluidly poetic way, and
sound and light add to the atmosphere.
'Once again, we stress the importance of
the screens, of their psychological influence
on those who are confronted with them,
on those who have to deal with their
permeability,' says Erwan. 'It's fascinating to
imagine lying on either side of such heavy
and imposing elements, which could be torn
apart within a few seconds.' — MM

**As part of a wider exhibition of the Bouroullecs' work,
17 Screens will appear at Frac Bretagne in Rennes,
France, from 25 March through 28 August 2016**
bouroullec.com

Extreme Makeover

Neri&Hu unites a segmented space with 'surgical implants' for fashion brand Comme Moi

Photos Dirk Weiblen

SHANGHAI — With a name like Comme Moi and a location in the French Concession area of Shanghai, Neri&Hu's recent retail offering sounds conspicuously European. In reality, though, it's the brainchild of Lu Yan, one of China's first-generation supermodels. Yan (34) called on the local design studio to produce a premier flagship worthy of its

young clientele – fans of fashion-forward logo-free garments. In a similar vein to Comme Moi clothing, the space relies on subtle branding.

Neri&Hu's signature raw-meets-refined aesthetic shines in the Art Deco Donghu Hotel. The site has seen multiple renovations and changes of use since its construction in 1925. Negotiating the traces of a building's motley past may challenge some, but it's what Neri&Hu does best. The designers liken their addition of new design elements to the historical interior to 'surgical implants that embody the Comme Moi brand'. Teamed with oak in certain areas, terrazzo flooring that moves up to form sales counter and seating also extends beyond the interior to confront passers-by. Once inside, shoppers are guided by a continuous rail. Snaking around corners and threading through the store's four rooms, it also provides structural support for Neri&Hu's custom-designed cabinetry. — TI

en.neriandhu.com

Tricks of
the Trade

Together with i29,
Frame surprised and
seduced visitors to
IMM LivingInteriors
with 'experience boxes'

Photos Ewout Huibers, courtesy of i29

COLOGNE — Let's be honest. Trade shows are not the sexiest (af)fairs. While kilometres of exhibition stands surely impress, when it comes to the art of seduction, most fall short. Tired of the standard 'show and tell' routine, *Frame* teamed up with Amsterdam-based architecture firm i29 at this year's IMM LivingInteriors show in an effort to break free from the mundane.

The expansive Frame pavilion, which consisted of five installations, showcased products from the industry's leading flooring and wallcovering brands. Housed in semi-translucent 'cubes' composed of high-quality foil mirrors by German brand Alluvial, the materials on display took to the stage in surreal scenes created by Dutch styling agency Kamer 465. The glossy exterior

of each 'experience box' reflected the surrounding fairgrounds and flirted with space and reality. Luring passers-by, flashing spotlights offered momentary glimpses of each exciting 'world'. Inside, mirrored walls further heightened the desired optical effect.

The installations, which highlighted three themes – Anything, Anywhere; Smart

Materials; and Inspired by Nature – featured work by renowned artists Heleen Blanken and Robbert de Goede, as well as designs by, among others, Diederik Schneemann, Dirk van der Kooij, and Jakob Schlaepfer. — MO
i29.nl
kamer465.nl

Billion-Dollar View

**El Equipo Creativo pumps up the luxury for
dockside restaurant OneOcean Club**

BARCELONA— The citizens of Barcelona are used to great – often abrupt – physical changes in their city. This is particularly true of the waterfront, Barcelona's greatest asset. Perhaps the acceptance of constant change explains the air of relative calm at Port Vell, the site of yet another physical and functional shift. New owners converted the Port Vell marina into an exclusive dock for the world's most expensive super yachts. A chic restaurant and cocktail bar near the sailing boats' mooring spot was part of the programme.

Situated in a purpose-built pavilion at the water's edge, OneOcean Club boasts an interior by El Equipo Creativo, the studio behind a handful of highly praised gastro-design projects, including Disfrutar and Ikibana. El Equipo Creativo has a knack for cleverly referencing both food and place. At Port Vell, terraces on either side of the dining room afford views of the billion-dollar boats, while a mirrored ceiling and glass façade draw the watery environment inside. Rich in materials, the dining room purrs with polished-brass elegance and curvaceous ↳

↰deep-blue seating. Golden frame-like columns draped with plants complement spiky hanging lamps that resemble coral. Both terraces, one of which accompanies the adjacent cocktail bar, are wrapped partially in bone-white brise-soleil screens. They are the work of Escofet 1886, a Catalan company that's pushed the boundaries of concrete since the time of Gaudí. Light filtering through the large perforated panels drenches the space in a fuzzy, dappled glow that enhances the drink-and-dine atmosphere. — SW

elequipocreativo.com

The dining room of El Equipo Creativo's OneOcean Club in Barcelona is soaked in subaqueous references. Spiky hanging lamps, for example, resemble coral.

Photo Fumio Araki

Web Shop

There's more to Moment's module for Me Issey Miyake than meets the eye

FUTAKO TAMAGAWA — Me Issey Miyake is one of numerous labels under the Japanese fashion designer's umbrella. At the time of writing, Miyake's T-shirt brand – launched in 2001 – had established 18 retail outlets across Japan. Responding to the company's desire to branch out and make the label appeal to younger customers, Tokyo-based studio Moment designed a fencelike structure for the display of prepackaged tees at a shopping complex in Futako Tamagawa.

Composed of an array of powder-coated-steel rods, each 6 mm in diameter, the system features horizontal elements that serve as hooks. Rods interlocked at angles, like a web of Scandinavian *himmeli* ornaments, form a self-supporting 3D module. As a partition, the structure also defines the brand's space, thus separating Me Issey Miyake from surrounding retailers in the busy complex.

While the outcome is practical – Moment had to come up with a structurally sound design using only a minimum of materials – the intricate web draws shoppers in for a closer look: an intriguing way to attract the punters. — KH

moment-design.com

With This Ring

A petite Boucheron product makes a grand spatial statement at the hands of Mathias Kiss

PARIS — Hovering like silvery clouds, a landscape of seven cubic clusters greeted visitors to Boucheron's Paris flagship on the Place Vendôme in December. Elaborating on his geometric vocabulary, Mathias Kiss used mirrors to reflect the nebular masses on walls and ceiling, creating Radiant Room's poetic, dreamy quality.

Located in a small room on the flagship's second floor, the intimate installation showcased Boucheron's new pink-gold Quatre Radiant ring, which Kiss displayed on a plinth. The 43-year-old designer – known for his strong artistic and architectural sensibilities – drew inspiration from the ring's *Clou de Paris* pattern, which evokes the *pavés*, or cobblestones, of the

Place Vendôme, which is home to the city's *haute joaillerie* stores.

In place for one month, the installation presented Boucheron's ring while evoking the greyness of the Parisian skies. Wrapped in silver leaf, individual cuboids stacked in sets of one to three formed cloudlike clusters while generating an interplay of volume and reflection. Some nestled into corners, while others protruded from walls.

The reinterpretation of traditional designs is a leitmotif in Kiss's work. Boucheron contacted him after discovering Froissé Mirror, a series of wall-mounted sculptures made up of creased and folded looking-glass shards. — AS

mathiaskiss.com

Con - sell - ation

Zodiac-inspired window displays lure customers into an astrological-inspired world at Selfridges

LONDON — Christmas time may be done and dusted, but Selfridges opted for an aesthetic with staying power for its holiday-season windows. As noted in *Frame* 108's coverage of Space Suite (p. 084), the galactic trend shows no signs of waning. Enter Selfridges, which jumped on the bandwagon with Journey to the Stars. The concept explored astrology and constellations, described by the retail firm's creative director, Linda Hewson, as 'timeless and relentlessly fascinating to so many people'.

Although the approach may not *seem* the least bit Christmassy, the in-house design team hatched the idea with the illustrious Star of Bethlehem in mind. Without a jingle bell or tinsel thread in sight, 12 windows captured the full spectrum of zodiac signs. Representing each symbol were metallic or glossy mannequins who flaunted custom headpieces crafted by various designers. Maiko Takeda – whose intricate work Björk ↳

↰ fans will recognize from the singer's Biophilia tour – made the equally elaborate crowns worn by an embracing couple in the Scorpio window. Emanating from the pair, a starburst of light accounted for just a fraction of the 450 m of fluorescent tubing used throughout the windows. While we're talking numbers, the displays also contained 10,000 laser-cut leaves and a whopping two tonnes of glitter.

Each star-sign interpretation was slick and polished, but the Selfridges team managed to squeeze in some humour, too. Taurus saw a horned figure trampling over a porcelain-littered floor – the proverbial bull in a china shop.

The windows continue Selfridges' strategy to steer customers into the store with artistic installations instead of products – a tactic it won't abandon anytime soon. 'Above all,' says Hewson, 'the theme gave us the opportunity to design startling displays, in-store experiences and product collaborations.' Catering to clientele who value doing over buying, the department store simultaneously opened Astrolounge, a 'mystical adult grotto' on its lower ground floor. Anyone interested in swapping their Santa stocking for a psychic reading or mystic workshop could be found there, counting their lucky stars. — TI

selfridges.com

The Taurus window at Selfridges in London referenced the proverbial bull in a china shop.

Enter the Matrix

The immersive world of online development
informs Stéphane Malka's office for Adyax

PARIS — 'People were coming in thinking it was a gallery,' says Stéphane Malka of his Parisian office for open-source company Adyax. In realizing a mobile space in which you rarely see people 'on the job', he's deliberately upping the ante in workplace design. Sitting at the entrance, Mufu (Mutant Furniture) marks this new frontier. A hybrid piece made from recycled timber, Mufu – 'either micro architecture or macro furniture', according to Malka – functions as both reception desk and seating yet also boasts a bed, phone booth, library and integrated bar.

In a play of perspective and spatial distortion, Malka's matrix system forms a series of dramatically different experiences over three levels, mirroring the immersive process of digital development. 'Adyax works on the web, with networks. The more they develop, the deeper they get. The further you get into the building, the further you advance into the network of cubes. It's both a physical and intellectual journey.' On one level, a corridor of 'golden windows' appears to float above Majorelle Blue flooring. The vivid colours, predominant in Middle Eastern architecture, suggest the moment when the sun sets over the sea, whereas the meditative layout of the space is a conscious reference to the transcendent properties of a church's nave. — **JP**

stephanemalka.com

Smoke and Mirrors

**C&C Design toys
with perception at
a Chinese trade fair**

GUANGZHOU — It may not have been modelled from a crumpled draft like the studio's previous pavilion for Guangzhou Design Week (*Frame* 104, p. 158), but C&C Design's installation for the 2015 edition of the event did echo the folded paper-like look of its predecessor. Visitors encountered a series of interconnected glass enclosures, some of which displayed projections. From within, viewers could flick their focus between a glass wall and the fairground beyond it – a space that was visible yet inaccessible from where they stood. The only way they could step outside the boundary was to retrace their footsteps.

To further obscure the audience's perception of space, C&C Design used laminated glass in a gradation of translucent to transparent, achieving an effect that doubled as a reference to China's smog-filled skies.

Entitled Haze, the installation conveyed a message of equally deep significance. The designers hoped to draw attention to what they call the invisible 'haze' surrounding society's obsession with the virtual world – the way we treat electronics like an extra limb and seem to have more screen time than face time (no, not the app). — TI
cocopro.cn

Get in Shape

A growing gym chain in London looks
to art and retail design for inspiration

Photos Gareth Gardner

LONDON — 'We're ditching the tired model and building destinations, not just gyms.' That's part of an announcement on 1Rebel's website. The nascent brand's second branch is located in the recently redeveloped Broadgate Circle, one of London's main business districts. Designed by up-and-coming practice Studio C102, the 800-m² basement – formerly occupied by mechanical systems and storage – looks more like a club than a gym, thanks to poured-concrete flooring and industrial-style detailing. In the words of Studio C102 principal Kyriakos Katsaros: 'The brief was to make each new 1Rebel gym as individualized as possible, while still keeping to the brand promise of every class feeling like a night out – an event in its own right rather than a means to an end.'

That explains why 1Rebel Broadgate is noticeably darker than its nearby predecessor at 63 St Mary Axe. 'By responding imaginatively to differences in the sites,' says Katsaros, 'we created a distinct sense of place for each. At the same time, we maintained a constant design language and an overall palette of materials, which draw inspiration from contemporary art and cutting-edge retail design rather than from the fitness sector.'

Features to look for include neon logos positioned behind dark-green welding curtains and a bespoke network of Kee ↳

Industrial-style detailing gives Studio C102's design for the latest 1Rebel gym a clubby air.

↰Klamp rails that weaves its way (almost seamlessly) around the front-of-house space and through the interiors. The network begins as a display of iPads whose images attract the attention of people passing the street-level shopfront. The rails then become a bench, form staircase balustrades and provide a simple rack for hanging the brand's sportswear range – only to end as seating again. Complementing a welcome desk finished in handcrafted white tiles is a black-tiled bar at the middle of the reception area, where patrons can pause for refreshments.

The building has two studios, notable for flooring made from recycled black rubber. Rumble is a circular space with rows of punchbags, and Reshape, which curves around the perimeter of the gym, contains benches and treadmills. Continuing the industrial feel, men's changing rooms have galvanized steel lockers, as opposed to copper-panelled lockers for women, and exposed copper pipes are perfect for heating towels. — **GG**

studio-c102.com

Focus Pocus

Architects 314 play with illusion for an eyewear store in Greece

CHALKIDA— It appears that no self-respecting retailer can do without a dedicated space in which customers can relax and socialize. Eyewear store C_29/Optimist in Chalkida, Greece, is no exception. If the vision-test procedure gets a bit much, customers can retreat to the courtyard at the rear of the shop for a spot of shuteye.

Architects 314 opted for consistent minimalism in the listed building, ensuring a transition from one room to another that is as seamless as possible. No matter whether you're in the front 'gallery' (trying on glasses), the laboratory (having your eyes tested and your frames adjusted) or the courtyard, the interior design hinges on the tension between rough and smooth, expressed succinctly in contrasting brickwork and glass.

Everything that isn't glass is whitewashed, from concrete floor to walls, and additional styling is restricted to a few strategically placed plants. It's all intended to make products the main spectacle – which they should be, if you can drag yourself out of the relaxation area. This climax to the retail experience contains a further sight for sore eyes: at first glance, the courtyard appears to be completely enclosed, yet the space is *en plein air*, thanks to a clever combination of black paint and poles that creates the illusion of containment. — WG

314architecturestudio.com

Photos Panagiotis Voumvakis

Plastic Politics

Dus hits pause on its widely publicized 3D-printed canal house to churn out a building befitting the Netherlands' EU presidency

Photos Ossip van Duivenbode

AMSTERDAM — When the Netherlands prepares for a presidency, not just any building will do. The opportunity to host a six-month-long assembly for the European Union's politicians called for an architectural statement that represents the now. On the same site that holds the ongoing 3D Print Canal House project, the architects at Dus put their skills to the test in a constructed version of the 100-yard dash. Capable of producing seamless objects up to 2 m wide and 3.5 m tall, Dus Architects' XXL printer paused from layering canal-house components to realize the outfit's first printed offspring to enter the public domain: the Europe Building.

The temporary structure, located in Amsterdam's historical Maritime District, is swathed in crisp white sails to illustrate the nation's nautical ways. Taking the definition of a curtain wall quite literally, the façade of sails effortlessly lifts to reveal an entrance flanked by 3D-printed bio-plastic seating. Fitted into triangulated alcoves, benches in EU-blue feature a textured parametric pattern that denotes the union's member states. During evening activities, aquamarine illumination surges across the building's translucent veil. After the conclusion of the presidency residency, the plastic elements will be tossed into the shredder for reuse. — LG

dusarchitects.com

Black Off

An's moody interior for clothing brand Heike lives in the shadows

HANGZHOU — Tucked away on the second floor of a furniture store in the Chinese city of Hangzhou, accessible only via a narrow staircase, Heike feels as if it's hiding in the shadows. The mood is further intensified by local outfit An's black-on-black interior, a melancholic palette explored in this issue's Frame Lab (page 176).

A futuristic UFO-like structure sits incongruously as a centrepiece in the sober concrete boutique. Perched on conical columns, the angular wood-and-metal volume accommodates fitting rooms, storage space and a small staff-only area. A similar yet much smaller structure ↳

↰ serves as a bar, helping to transform the store into a venue equipped to host art and design exhibitions.

Although glass runs along three sides of the 200-m² shop, much of the light entering through the windows is dampened by suspended clothing displays. Heike's monochromatic merchandise hangs from backlit panels, an effect that's duplicated by black wall-mounted luminaires elsewhere in the store. Lighting elements, clothes hangers and mirrors were all custom designed for the project. — TI

wengshanwei.com

A wood-and-metal structure at the centre of Heike accommodates fitting rooms, storage space and a private area for staff.

RETAIL THERAP

Poised to give KaDeWe Berlin a makeover, Vittorio Radice discloses how he's been transforming dull department stores into sexy shopping magnets for over 20 years.

WORDS *Robert Thiemann* **PORTRAITS** *Juliane Eirich*

IST

Vittorio

We plan to meet a few days before Christmas in Milan at La Rinascente, a department store where I find thousands of men, women and children crowding the aisles in their search for holiday gifts. In the seventh-floor food hall, shoppers jostle as they order espressos and shove their way into My Sushi or Obikà Mozzarella, while enjoying a fantastic view of the Duomo di Milano, almost within fingertip distance.

Vittorio Radice strides into the clamorous Maio Restaurant, catches sight of my worried look and suggests we retreat to a quiet meeting room in the building's rear office. We walk through nondescript corridors lined with racks and boxes – remarkable how different the front and back offices of a fashionable department store can be. As we move along, Radice has a friendly word for everyone passing by.

It's obvious that my tall companion – well over 180 cm, native of Northern Italy, mid-50s, pale-blue shirt, dark-blue suit – has a winning manner that doesn't go unnoticed. It's a quality that's undoubtedly helped him to transform one department store after another, beginning in the 1990s. When British furniture chain Habitat lay at death's door, he revived the organization and arranged for it to be sold to Ikea. He turned stiff-upper-lip Selfridges into a swinging retail emporium and supervised the metamorphosis of Moscow's luxurious TsUM. But when his magic failed to work for Marks & Spencer, he was forced to move aside within a year. Two new store concepts intended to symbolize his vision of the multinational's future were publicly rejected. It was a misadventure that didn't stop the owners of La Rinascente from working with Radice since 2005, however, as they closed certain stores and had him make others into thriving contemporary shopping magnets. Like so many department stores, the old-fashioned Italian chain required a major overhaul. ↵

'PEOPLE WILL RETURN TO DEPARTMENT STORES THAT ARE SEXY AND RELEVANT'

VITTORIO RADICE

1957
Born in Como, Italy

1990
Buying director, Habitat International

1992
Managing director, Habitat International

1996
Managing director, Selfridges

1998
CEO, Selfridges

2003
Executive director, M&S Home Group

2005 – Present
Vice chairman, La Rinascente

2013
Acquisition, Illum Copenhagen

2015
Acquisitions, Alsterhaus Hamburg, KaDeWe Berlin and Oberpollinger Munich

Independent director, YOOX Net-A-Porter Group

Vittorio Radice leads the European expansion of Thailand-based Central Group.

OMA's KaDeWe Overhaul

Vittorio Radice tasked Rem Koolhaas's OMA with the renovation of historical Berlin department store KaDeWe, which recently came under the ownership of La Rinascente. To make the 63,000-m² shopping area comprehensible, the designers divided the vast space into quarters to create what they refer to as 'easily accessible and navigable components – similar to distinct urban sectors embedded in a unified city fabric'. The project is a reaction to shifting consumer behaviours and to the changes that online retail has inflicted on the traditional department-store model. KaDeWe's customers should expect the wow factor that Radice says was lacking in the original building.

oma.eu

The insertion of four atria and the creation of German-style quarters will make KaDeWe's expansive interior more digestible for shoppers.

A rendering shows one of the four atria included in OMA's renovation; rising through the void is a clever configuration of escalators that offers the impression of a traditional spiral staircase when viewed from above.

'DON'T MAKE IT SO DIFFICULT TO SHOP; MAKE IT AS EASY AS POSSIBLE'

Before and after: KaDeWe's renovation will include the elevation of part of the roof and the extension of food halls to incorporate a terrace.

↰ **All over the world, department stores are struggling to stay afloat. In recent years, famous chains like Sears and Target have closed dozens of outlets. In the Netherlands, national chain V&D announced bankruptcy on the last day of 2015. Soon after that, Macy's said it would close no fewer than 40 stores. When making comparisons with other options – I'm thinking of online giant Amazon, fast-fashion outfits like H&M and Primark, discounters like T.J. Maxx – consumers call department stores boring, mediocre, expensive and inconvenient. How did it get to this?** VITTORIO RADICE: You have to go back to the origins of department stores, to the likes of Le Bon Marché in 1850. They brought new products and new techniques into what was basically a vertical market over several floors. Their idea of shopping was not only about buying. It was also about spending a couple of hours away from home without having to leave town. People who used to go to the church when they had a spare hour began going to the department store to see something new. Everyone wanted to participate in the spectacle of buying and seeing others buy.

The introduction of the escalator gave pace to shopping. It sounds like a banal thing, but this way of moving from one floor to another and seeing new environments, displays and stacks of products excited people. That's when mass consumption started.

The late 1970s saw the rise of specialist store chains with a broader assortment; the focus was on product instead of environment and on competitive pricing. Department stores became detached from their origins, from a time of showing new and beautiful things in a well-designed environment and offering great service. Instead they entered a price war with specialist chains and failed.

Top-segment department stores are trying to turn the tide by making some wise investments. How does that strategy work at Rinascente? People will return to department stores that are sexy and relevant. When I arrived here in 2005, we had 20 stores. Many were just selling products and had to compete on price. We determined which stores could successfully face the future: those in beautiful buildings with prime locations in touristic cities. We closed eight stores that didn't meet our criteria and started refurbishing the rest to give them the dignity they once had.

In Milan we had plastic flooring and low windows with heavy shutters. Everything was dark. There was no joy. So we made the windows higher, used bulletproof glass, removed the shutters, and changed the direction of the escalators to facilitate traffic.

In 2006 we brought in interesting brands – popular brands with a focus on design, material and price. Our job is limited to editing: we decide the best way to design and use space,

Collection Versus Chain

RADICE: 'In the 20th century, department store chains developed nationally. But today we see more commonality linking stores in Milan, London and Paris than those in Milan, Piacenza and Parma. So it makes sense for Rinascente to close stores in smaller Italian cities and bland locations and to acquire stores like Illum in Copenhagen and KaDeWe in Berlin, which are better than national chains when it comes to gathering tourists together and working out collaborations with brands. Currently, it's smarter to build a *collection* of stores, each in a landmark building at a prime location in a tourist destination, than a *chain* of stores. Each store in the *collection* should be one of a kind, a tourist attraction dedicated to the city it's in.'

and we select brands that together can create one voice. In some department stores, the ensemble lacks a single voice. Too many voices, too little coherence and people can't hear you – you don't stand for anything.

In 2008 we added a very important thing: the food hall. Until then, the rule had been: we don't do food, too complicated. By opening the top floor – previously a depot for unused fixtures – with terraces that let visitors almost touch the cathedral, we became *the* store of Milan instead of just one of 20 Rinascente stores in Italy.

The following year we opened a design supermarket. Milan is famous for design, but there hadn't been a place that offered a collection of such products under one roof. Because of the food hall with its terraces and the design supermarket, we could add 'Milano' to the shopping bag under the Rinascente logo and be detached from the chain. We will do the same in Florence, Rome and Turin. Each of our stores will have a unique look. It's much harder work, but in Milan the turnover is nearly four times what it was when we started – and we left the historical building intact. It's all about continually changing the interior, the brands, the events and so on. You cannot stop.

Do you need to be in the top segment to be successful with this type of approach? Or can a mid-segment department store adopt the same strategy? I think so. When your store attracts ten million people, as ours does, you have to welcome everybody. The visitor who can only afford a glass of water today may be drinking champagne tomorrow. The important thing is to sell both with the same spirit. The customer who spends one euro still receives a piece of luxury. The success of the modern department store is high quality for everyone.

How does a mid-segment store without top brands offer high quality? Forget plastic dishes; serve that sandwich on a ceramic plate. It will taste better. Don't make your customers feel as if they're the poorest people in the world. Go that extra mile regarding attitude, service, design and marketing. When Target introduced its red-dot logo, people went there because it looked cool on their shopping bags.

Luxury brands are opening lots of stores around the world, a move that gives them maximum control and high margins. But each outlet has to express the brand's DNA, so they all look alike, and that can get boring. What advice do you have for them? They will negate this, but they all follow the leader. When a brand is successful with a zipper, with high windows or with a particular location, others will follow. We'll end up with a community in which everything looks the same if we're not careful.

How do you differentiate in a mass market? After all, when your sales numbers get into the billions, you're undeniably serving a mass market. I strongly believe you have to ↰

DENSERVICE

OMER SERVICE

Radice's Department-Store Commandments

1 — Don't push product out by discounting
2 — Focus on getting people in
3 — Restore dignity
4 — Give space and freedom to a curated mix of attractive brands
5 — Show something new every 4 m
6 — Hire architects and designers to create a singular voice
7 — Participate in local culture
8 — Treasure the musician that's playing in front of your store
9 — Sell products strongly linked to the city you're in
10 — Have the guts to try something unconventional

↰dedicate your store to the community you're in. If someone from Paris or New York shops in Katmandu, they should have the feeling that product, service and store are dedicated to Katmandu. You can achieve this by participating in the local culture and behaving like a local store. This is what we've been advocating for years.

In China, some luxury brands have built huge façades in front of existing buildings, disrespecting history and alienating themselves from the fabric of the city. Their voice automatically becomes weaker, because they've lost the integrity people expect from them. Potential customers recognize what's been done to the original architecture and to their roots. They're finding it more difficult to enter these monstrosities. The building itself doesn't belong to the brand, which is only the caretaker.

You asked Rem Koolhaas to rethink KaDeWe Berlin, a store recently acquired by the owners of La Rinascente. What are the plans? The biggest problem at KaDeWe is a lack of wow. You don't see the escalators upon arrival, and you have no appreciation of the size of the 63,000-m² shopping area awaiting you. To make this huge space digestible, we will insert four atria and create German-style quarters – so not as pure and elegant as they would be in Paris. We'll use the clash that the war caused in Berlin, where old buildings sit next to new ones in a mix of styles and materials. The customer should be able to read the store at a glance and find it easy to circulate. We will lift part of the roof and extend the food halls to realize a terrace. KaDeWe's food halls are world famous. The store takes pride in the fact that they carry 980 German sausages. The statement itself makes them a hero in my eyes. And since German cars are also world renowned, KaDeWe ought to have four or five car showrooms.

Many department stores are adopting the strategy you employ. Many make soup, but with different ingredients. Many follow the rules that the market dictates. What's missing is the guts to do something new and naughty that hasn't been tried before. Unusual advertising, loud music, specific materials, the participation of artists and musicians. Will it work for us to sponsor a boxing match or a car race? We need to get away from conventional thinking – to stop putting Gucci next to Dolce & Gabbana and Prada next to Vuitton to make a nice line-up that's meant to attract customers. We have to stop thinking like that.

Cosmetics, jewellery and watches occupy the ground floor of every luxury department store. Is it necessary to break that mould? Yes, but we need courage to do it. I once gave a lecture in New York. At Heathrow I was confronted with Chanel, Dior and Estée Lauder. The inflight magazine featured exactly the same brands. Upon arrival at JFK: same brands. At the local department store: there they were again. I'd had

enough. And I had the topic of my talk as well. Next year we'll refurbish our Florence branch, and cosmetics will go to the basement. [Laughs out loud.] It's an act of courage, because cosmetics are not only very expensive but also sold in very small spaces. To prevent boredom, you have to stimulate visitors by showing them something new every 4 m. An average cosmetics counter is 3 m long and is staffed by one or two people, because of the value of the product.

Last year 10 Corso Como was on the brink of bankruptcy. Why do concept stores get in trouble? The 1,000-m² concept store often plays in a remote location. Our 30,000-m² store plays on Piazza Duomo. Concept stores curate jackets, but we edit brands. Department stores play the game at a higher level. Each of our floors is comparable to a concept store, but those participating are the brands themselves. We give them the freedom they want. Want to paint your wall red? Do it. Want to sell that jacket for €3,000. Go ahead. We provide the location and generate traffic. That's it.

'YOU HAVE TO DEDICATE YOUR STORE TO THE COMMUNITY YOU'RE IN'

What would you advise concept stores? From the standpoint of the consumer rather than the retailer: you're not embracing the customer enough. The good ones smile at you at the door. An example in Berlin is Andreas Murkudis, which sells beautiful products but isn't fussy about them. You're invited to handle the wallets and shoes without having to worry about it. Others are simply too precious about their merchandise. So make your store as accessible as possible. Mix the Nike sneaker you selected with that €10,000 cashmere coat. Don't make it so difficult to shop; make it as easy as possible.

How should design labels be selling furniture these days? It's a small world, the world of design. Only 0.5 per cent of the population speaks the same language; the rest don't talk about design. Cassina, for instance,

is an established company, but very few people have heard of it. Cassina constantly concentrates on making beautiful products but spends nothing on communication. It's like pushing water uphill. You should automatically think of Cassina when you want to buy a sofa, but not many people do. Another reason is the focus on designers rather than manufacturers, although the latter pay the bills. We may know all about the designer of a piece without knowing who makes it and where to buy it.

Design brands need to stop and think – to determine how to sell before deciding what to make or which designer to use. Furniture manufacturers should have been the first retailers to go online. They should offer something like a car configurator to help visitors choose from the various options. And they need to get their names out there in much the same way as BMW and Mercedes have done.

But those carmakers are much bigger companies. You have to ask yourself: why are furniture companies so small? Why is their profile so high and their volume so low? Probably the biggest company in Italy is Natuzzi. Do you know any designer who works for them? Probably not, but you do know that Natuzzi stands for sofas. If you go downstairs and ask people if they know Gucci, they'll say yes. But nobody will be able to name Gucci's creative director, Alessandro Michele. They won't know who's been designing for Gucci during the past ten years. I'm not even sure they'll remember that Tom Ford designed for Gucci 15 years ago.

Buying products is gradually being replaced by 'sharing' and 'experiencing'. Do you see these trends affecting department stores? For sure. We are researching the possibilities of souvenirs and handicrafts as a way of dedicating our stores to their locations. We want to give exposure to local talent: young artisans skilled in bookbinding, pottery or even shoe repair. Some time ago we hosted a popular event that highlighted the lost tradition of repairing things like bicycles and watches. We're also discussing a series of souvenirs with a strong link to location – like socks or biscuits made in Milan by small, specialized factories.

We're back in the noisy food hall saying our goodbyes. Radice tells me I'd be surprised to know how many people drop into the store at least once a week, often during a 15-minute break: 'They see hundreds of people moving up the escalator and want to follow them to the seventh floor, with its terraces overlooking the cathedral. Still feeling excited, they spot a handbag, tie or suit on the way down, and they buy it. Not because of its function, but as a souvenir of their visit.'

I watch as he disappears into the crowd, on the way to join his wife and buy gifts for the holidays. ✕

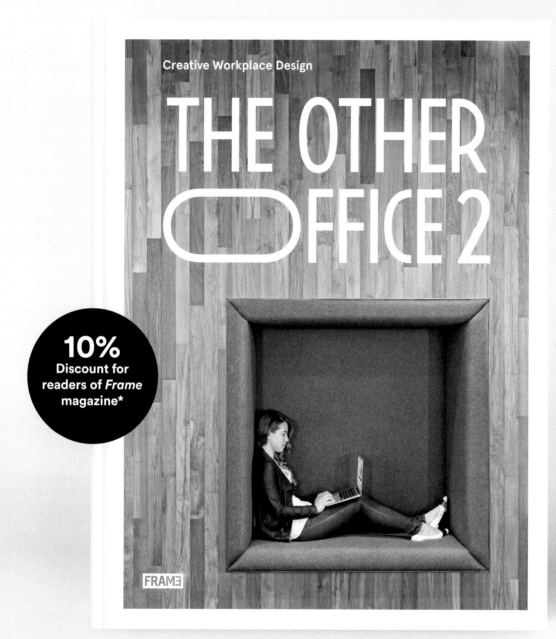

COLOUR

Most healthcare spaces have a sterile appearance, dominated by pristine whites and cool blues. But current technologies allow designers to take a more chromatic approach to clinics, hospitals and the like. In this issue's Frame Lab, we take a comprehensive look at the restorative and uplifting benefits of colour.

Comprehendi

Colour contrast is everything claims Hilary Dalke, who's applied her know-how to everything from prisons and hospitals to railway stations.

WORDS *Jonathan Openshaw* PORTRAITS *Anna Huix*

g Colour

TALKING colour theory with Professor Hilary Dalke is far from black and white, and any attempt to link particular colours with certain moods is given short shrift. 'That's one of my big beefs with colour psychology,' she says. 'People constantly ask whether red makes you feel passionate or yellow makes you more creative. Well, I'm sorry, but you're not going to get someone who has worked with scientists for three decades across academic research and commercial consultancy to back that one.'

Dalke approaches colour as more of a recipe than a set of isolated elements. Just as a chef looks at a bag of ingredients and sees a potential dish waiting to be made, Dalke sees the human response to a colour as emerging through contrast with other colours and environmental factors. 'It's less about red being warm and blue being cool, and more about combinations having different levels of impact,' she says. 'You very rarely see colour in isolation. You can have the most beautiful grey vista in a room, but put a single stripe of yellow there and the whole space will take on a purple tinge. If you're in a single-colour environment, you'll soon become totally unaware of the colour. Contrast is everything.'

Her complex understanding of applied colour has been gained over a career that combines, as mentioned, funded academic research, commercial consultancy and trend forecasting. Having established the Colour Design Research Centre at London Southbank University in the 1990s, Dalke moved to the city's Kingston University in 2003, where she drove collaborations with leading institutions, including the Universities of Oxford, Reading and Cambridge. She has worked with a variety of clients, ranging from the NHS to Transport for London, and is the founder of Cromocon,

an organization specializing in, among other things, better accessibility of public space by means of colour coding.

Like all human senses, sight is influenced by nature *and* nurture, making the study of colour and wellbeing incredibly complex. On the one hand, the perception of colour has a biological basis. The human eye has two channels for receiving and processing visual information: rod cells, which control the perception of light and dark and focus on tones and movement, and cone cells, which react to red-green-blue (RGB) colours. We also know there is a strongly inherited aspect to colour perception, with men being around 16 times more likely than women to be colour-blind.

The biology of sight reveals a lot about the human response to colour. Blue, for instance, is the most popular colour globally, regardless of culture. This might be due to how quickly blue recedes from the visual field. Blue-sensitive cone cells are outnumbered by yellow receptors 20 to one, and only two per cent of them perceive blue, which is subsequently one of the least stimulating colours. This goes some way in explaining why blue cars are more likely to be involved in accidents. Yellow, however, elicits one of the strongest responses in the human eye. It is the first colour that newborn babies can see. When international orange (a mix of yellow and red) showed up in North American industrial regulations, it reduced factory fatalities by 18 per cent. Why? Because that shade of orange was found to retain its visibility from the farthest distance at midday.

'You need to have a deep understanding of how the eye works if you're going to begin untangling the human response to colour,' says Dalke. 'But it's about much more than that. There's a very strong cultural aspect, and ↳

Applying colour is not about making the place 'nicer' but about making it more effective

⌐even in these globalized times you can look at an interiors magazine and make a pretty good guess about where a certain palette comes from.' Whether you see the muted palette of Scandinavia, the vivid hues of the Provence or the raw natural materials of Latin America, regional variations are pronounced.

This heady combination of the culturally relative and the biologically universal explains the profound impact that colour can have on people. In the Trobriand Islands of Papua New Guinea, traditional seafaring communities even used colour in a kind of psychological warfare. In his seminal work on the social systems of the South Pacific, early 20th-century anthropologist Bronisław Malinowski wrote that the densely patterned canoe prow boards were far more than decorative.

Painted red, white and black – three colours that appear in almost every human culture *and* language – the prow boards have been compared to Celtic designs or the optical art of Bridget Riley. When viewed from the beach, though, an approaching flotilla of lurid Trobriand canoes had a powerfully disorientating effect, particularly on rival communities that had very little chromatic variation in a blue expanse of sky and sea. The islanders used the prow boards to 'bedazzle' their enemy and to gain the upper hand in trade or warfare. Similarly powerful psychological effects were reported in the popular phantasmagoria of Victorian England, where candlelight and mirrors were used to overexcite the senses and induce effects comparable to those produced by powerful psychotropic drugs.

The strong link between visual stimulation and human psychology underpins much of Dalke's work and explains why she was approached by Her Majesty's

Prison Service (HMPS) to revamp prison units. 'Working on prisons was particularly interesting,' she says, citing the challenge inherent in the view that 'people are there to be punished, so why should we make the place nicer?' Her great success lay in demonstrating that a stark, sensory-deprived prison actually leads to a regression in inmates' behaviour and an increase in suicide and self-harm. Applying colour was not about making the place 'nicer' but about making it more effective. Using different colour strategies between connected spaces – such as cell and association area – raised some prisoners' spirits.

Dalke has undertaken 12 prison-unit redesigns for HMPS, making some powerful discoveries along the way, such as the fact that the peak suicide time of 4 p.m. can be addressed by considering natural light levels and colour ambience in cells during the late afternoon. One of the best vindications of her work came in a follow-up visit to a women's suicide and self-harm prison unit: 'The staff wanted to show me the showers and seemed very excited about it,' she recalls. 'So I went to have a look and couldn't see anything different. Instead of the traditional white tiles, we'd created a tile pattern with stripes of white, warm rose and beige, but they looked exactly the same – and that's what the guards were so excited about. They usually had a huge problem with inmates smashing tiles for use in suicide attempts, and after six months the new showers were completely intact.' Dalke's subtle change appeared to have impressed users, who recognized the care and thought that had gone into the refurbishment.

Armed with compelling proof of how colour and contrast can increase a feeling of wellbeing and alter human behaviour, Dalke set up Cromocon in 2003. Besides colour-coding for public spaces, the organization

caters for visually impaired people (VIPs). One project is a meter for measuring the light reflectance value (LRV) of materials, text or objects; a digital app calculates the contrast in any given environment and makes it visible. Previous research revealed that numerous public facilities, such as Paddington Station, were invisible to as many as one-quarter of VIPs. Cromocon's work in this area informs legislation at a national and international level; examples of clients are the British Standards Institution and the American National Standards Institute.

Dalke's next mission is to ensure a greater understanding of relationships between colour, contrast and wellbeing. It is important for all designers and architects, not just those working with special-needs groups. 'There is still a reluctance to access tools and guidance, and many designers believe such aids limit their creativity. It doesn't need to be that way.' Nike's Zoom Soldier 8 FlyEase shoe is a good example of how a product that was inspired by physical disability can be beneficial to all. Designed in response to a letter to Nike – from a young man suffering from cerebral palsy whose limited motor function made it impossible for him to put on a Nike trainer without help – the new FlyEase has a zippered heel and large easy-to-fasten straps. Nike is best known for collaborating with able-bodied celebrities, such as basketball player LeBron James, but this new design challenge led to innovations that wouldn't have come about otherwise.

'I think all people – able-bodied or not – feel much more comfortable in environments that work well,' concludes Dalke. The subtle nuances of colour and the impact it can have on human psychology and wellbeing are often missed by non-disabled designers and architects, but the work that people like Dalke put into special-needs projects is bringing the importance of colour to the fore. 'It's often hard for us to articulate how we feel about colour, because it's such a direct and powerful experience. Designers and architects need to be far more strategic in the way they deploy colour and contrast in built environments.' ✕

kingston.ac.uk
cromocon.com

Five health-boosting interiors explore the effect of colour on physical and mental wellbeing.

WORDS *Shonquis Moreno*

TAKE THE CURE

Turquoise curtains enclose treatment
rooms with floor-to-ceiling glass walls.

Jean de Lessard's pastel interior
for Uniprix Kieu Truong is meant
to humanize the pharmacy.

Photos Adrien Williams

Soft Touch
Pharmacy

Montreal designer Jean de Lessard paints abstract
interior landscapes that mix form with feng shui, and
composition with colour. His palette for pharmacy Uniprix
Kieu Truong is both pale and powerful. The large open-
plan space benefits from a single coherent scheme.
'We used pastels to manage the Yin and Yang of this
joyful client,' says the designer. The white retail space
features shelving in mint and pink, salmon tables with
mirrored storage bases, butter-yellow walls and baby-
blue counters. Treatment rooms have radiused floor-
to-ceiling glass walls, pastel curtains and blond wood
surfaces. These colours make the pharmacy 'empathetic'
and unpretentious, inviting instead of clinical, and to
get its complexion just right, De Lessard's team custom-
fabricated the pink-peach laminate. 'We tried to make it
as human and as simple as possible,' he says. 'We want
clients to feel *good* here, to face no major disruptions,
to feel that they are in a human and colourful space with
almost no design.' De Lessard peered through a feng shui
lens – noting north, south, east and west – when planning
the layout of the shop and drew in a maximum of natural
light to give the surfaces a burnish. Then he mounted
fluorescent strips, each 61 cm wide, flush with the ceiling
to further illuminate the vista below; together they form
a radiant, albeit unobtrusive and gentle, sun. ↳
delessard.com

High-Profile Hues
Pop-up gym

↰ Forget grief, forget death: black is the (slimming) colour of elegance and exclusivity. In a hush-hush-but-high-profile New York 'showroom' for sportswear giant Nike, which opened in April 2015, invitation-only guests work out with celebrity fitness models and enjoy both performance analysis and personalized tailoring. A cross between gym and boutique, the Nike+ 45 Grand pop-up – which occupies the two floors of a former metal workshop in SoHo – is designed by Rafael de Cárdenas (*Frame* 103, p. 132) in collaboration with creative director Jen Brill. Theirs is a warm but strong approach to femininity: the central studio, in shades of black and grey, can be converted from workout area to display room, while clients entering the skylit mezzanine above found themselves in a lounge featuring powder-puff-pink banquettes, exposed wooden roof beams and a herringbone floor. The pop-up is a veritable celebration of structure, material, contrast and *colour*. At the time of writing, its closing date is yet to be confirmed. ↳

architectureatlarge.com

Photos David Allee

A rounded wall of frosted-acrylic fins illuminated by alternating hues – pink, purple and blue – allows daylight to penetrate Nike+ 45 Grand. The speed at which the colours change corresponds to activities inside, as well as to the time of day.

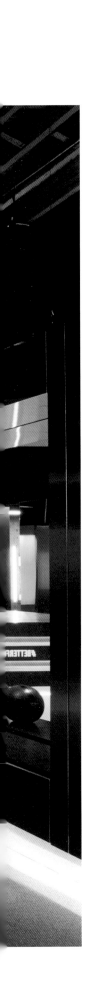

Photo David Allee

The comfort of a boudoir welcomes
guests to a skylit mezzanine lounge
at Nike+ 45 Grand with furnishings in
a powder-puff-pink upholstery fabric:
Divina MD 613 from Kvadrat.

Zoom+ picked an intense blue for its logo and interiors, a colour that refers to healing and relaxation.

Photos Boone Speed

Positive Energy
Care clinic

↰ Seemingly a fusion of cosmetics boutique, coffee shop and Google office, Zoom+Care is a clinic in Oregon that turned itself from a series of urgent-care clinics into an on-demand, smart phone-activated 'retail care system' that aims to give individuals control of their own healthcare. The organization used colour to broadcast the change, which included the creation of Zoom+Labs, described as 'performance-based primary care studios'. In these spaces, tests that determine the health of body and brain are used to calibrate wellness programmes that involve traditional and nontraditional medicines, food and exercise. Based on the frequent appearance of blue in brand identities to convey trust, reliability and stability – and in healthcare to promote calm, healing and relaxation – the prevalence of Zoom+Blue conveys the increasing good health of the brand throughout its transition. Zoom+ chose a particularly intense, highly saturated blue to set its innovations apart from the industry status quo. Secondary palettes and illustrations used elsewhere allude to high performance levels and healthy eating, while helping to distinguish the brand's product lines. Neon orange, red and magenta fill Zoom+Labs with a dynamic ambience. In Zoom+Prime areas, where food and movement regimens are used to treat chronic conditions, three shades of green emphasize the importance of healthy eating. Colours and illustrations in spaces for children take their cues from storybooks. ↳

zoomcare.com

Vibrant colours like neon orange give
Zoom+Labs an athletic, dynamic ambience.

**Following colour zones introduced by MVSA
Architects, Tinker Imagineers created interactive
experiences to distract and entertain patients at
the Juliana Children's Hospital.**

Photo Wim Verbeek

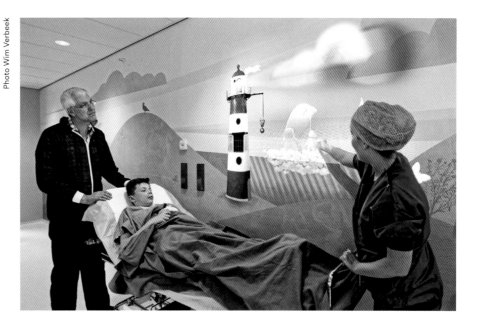

Photo Michael van Oosten

Soothing Treatment
Children's hospital

↰ Happiness design? To comfort and delight ailing children, a hospital in The Hague greets patients with a rich but simple palette that ties together architecture, furnishings, signage, wallcoverings and multimedia. MVSA Architects, part of the VolkerWessels Consortium, is responsible for both the exterior and interior design of the HagaHospital, which includes the Juliana Children's Hospital. The firm established four colour zones (green, yellow, purple and blue) that are used for walls, furnishings and doorways and that relate to wayfinding and functionality. Experience-design agency Tinker Imagineers added wall graphics and interactive media to MVSA's colour-coded zones. The interior design is crisp, clean and white, and the animations are full of character, literally. 'It is not just 4,000 m² of animated wallpaper,' says Tinker's Stan Boshouwers. 'Via interactive projections and animations layered over wallcoverings in treatment rooms, the pre-op room and the passageway to the operating theatre, the storytelling follows five characters who live in a world of sun, sand and sea – and who accompany young patients on their journey through the hospital.' The colour scheme helps to define each character's personality. Computerlike C-Bot, for example, is grass-green, 'an eye-catching but quieting shade', Boshouwers says, 'because most children are scared of hospital machines'. C-Bot is rational and technical but optimistic, smart and ever-curious about medical devices, mediating between them and the children whose lives depend on them. Colours are characters in this interior, design tools that almost make illness another part of the adventure, a rite of passage on the way to the operating room. ↳

mvsa-architects.com
tinker.nl

Photos Rod Borland

Light Work(out)
Gym

↰ 'I'm actually quite colour-blind, so we winged it a lot,' says Core Collective founder Jason de Savary, playfully understating colour's contribution to his UK gym interiors, for which Waind Gohil + Potter Architects did the overall interior design. De Savary opted for a warm, 'ungym-like', rather gentlemen's-clubby atmosphere – in contrast to the typical fitness space with its 'painful strip lighting'. 'Colour in the studio gives us the flexibility to change the feel of the whole space in an instant,' he explains. 'People have rigorous workout regimes, so we thought it would add to their routine to be surprised by the changing space.' To reach his goal, De Savary not only brings in regular rotations of art from The Dot Project Gallery; he also hired lighting designer Alexander Stileman and Knektd to give each studio multiple personalities. In general, studies have proved that reds and similar hues are perceived as stimulants. Stileman's scheme affects clients at different points throughout their workouts: warm and hot reds at the beginning of a class shift into calming blues, for example, during the post-workout cool-down period. 'The system is infinitely programmable,' Stileman says, 'and is regularly changed to suit different trainers and workouts.' The lighting is moody, not bright (except for invigorating bursts during spin classes), and all tinctured light is indirect, avoiding shades like green that distort skin tones. Direct light sources – high-CRI LEDs – make gym members appear to be 'in the pink' at all times. ✕

core-collective.co.uk
wgpa.co.uk
stilemanlighting.com
knektd.co.uk

Lighting at Core Collective adapts to the different activity levels during a workout.

SUBMERGED

Chromatic concepts challenge objective reality and perceptual boundaries.

WORDS *Floor Kuitert*

For her installation, *Yellowbluepink*, Ann Veronica Janssens filled the entire interior at London's Wellcome Collection with a dense and disorientating multicoloured mist.
wellcomecollection.org

Photo Laurids Gallée

'Perceiving colours at certain times of the day affects both energy levels and mood': Éléonore Delisse comments on the design of her Day and Night Lamp, a remedy for seasonal affective disorder.
eleonoredelisse.com

THE IMMERSIVE experience. An absolute must for the survival of those in the retail and hospitality sectors. Engaging your clientele has never been more important. But in a world congested with stimuli, how can you stand out? Digital technologies enable us to add extra dimensions to physical space, and virtual reality can even conjure a simulated personal presence, but none of the above satisfies the desire for a more direct bodily experience.

Enhancing – and sometimes even expanding – objective reality with experiential analogue layers, designers address the persistent need for out-of-this-world encounters. Hovering on the edge of our perceptual boundaries are designs that trick the eye. Chromatic lighting alters the sense of space, afterimages reveal colours that differ from the originals, and multihued patterns give rise to optical illusions; all play on both the limitations and the strengths of the eye's photoreceptor cells.

Well-known artists – such as American James Turrell and Danish-Icelandic Olafur Eliasson – have paved the way for years. Currently, the aesthetic language of their optically intriguing concepts is finding its way into pop culture, with Canadian rapper Drake's 'Hotline Bling' clip featuring a setting that is strikingly similar to some of Turrell's work. Although the 'light wizard' had nothing to do with Drake's production, speculations about a collaboration between rapper and artist exposed the latter's colourful projects to a wide and unexpected audience. And, as seen before, when art exits the gallery and starts influencing our more immediate surroundings, surprising things can happen. ✕

Photo courtesy of Mary Katrantzou

The optically illusive patterns adorning Mary Katrantzou's A/W 2016 collection are reminiscent of psychedelic prints from the 1960s. marykatrantzou.com

The 'light-shaping' surfaces that CSM
graduate Jordan Söderberg Mills
creates rely on white light to generate
colour, form and pattern.
soderbergmills.com

Photo courtesy of Arnout Meijer Studio

Visitors to Dutch Invertuals' No Static exhibition walked through Arnout Meijer's orange-lit tunnel, 16 Feet of Twilight, and marvelled at the 'blue screen' afterimage as they exited the installation.
arnoutmeijer.nl

Tijs Gilde's Fringe – a flexible partition for open-plan workspaces – is a hanging panel of Luxaflex strips whose colours are mixed in an 'analogue' way.
tijsgilde.com

The results may seem manipulated, but architect
and photographer Erin O'Keefe's still-life series,
Natural Disasters, is based on an analogue
treatment of multi-layered, spatial scenes.
erinokeefe.com

Chromatic lighting alters the sense of space and multihued patterns give rise to optical illusions

Tokyo, a work by Matt Vial, conveys the
artist's search for 'the relationship between
minimal space and vibrant lighting'.
m a t t v i a l . c o m

'In my work, rules of perspective, distance,
and light are bent. Space can become a
solid object, and places are folded on top
of one another,' says Adam Friedman, the
artist behind *The Nature of Inquiry #2.*
a r t b y a d a m f r i e d m a n . c o m

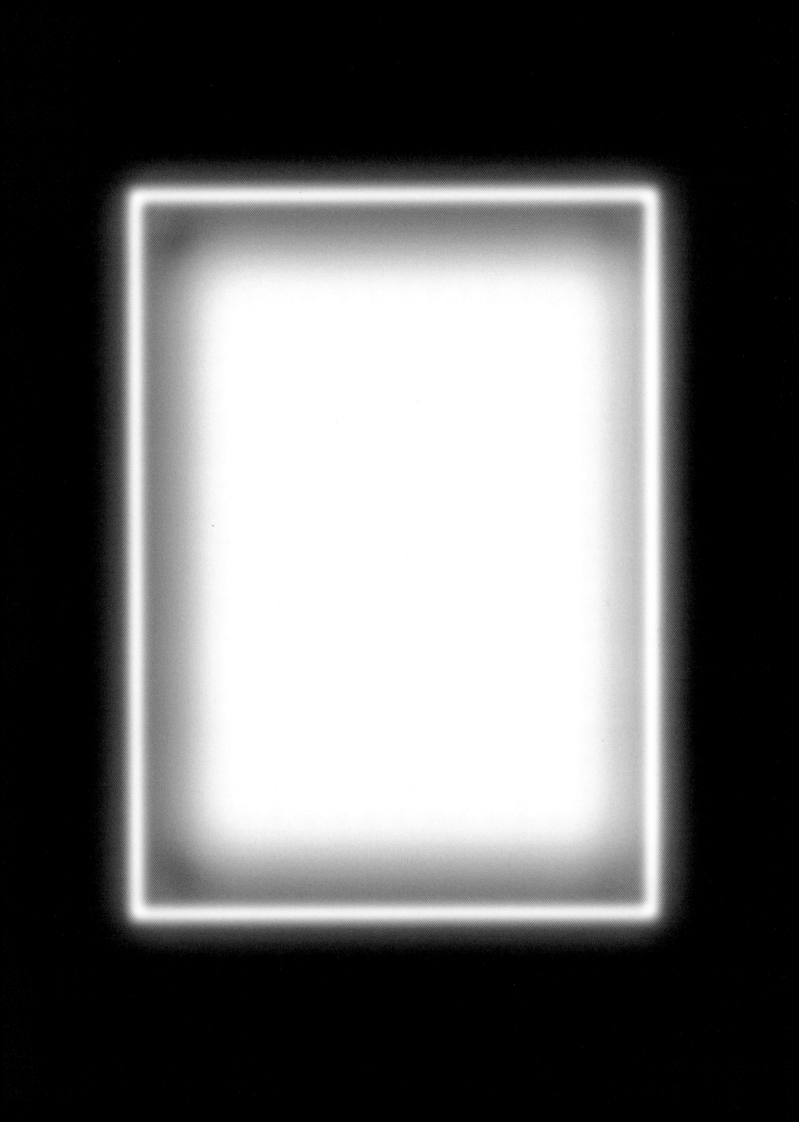

Rachel Harding uses diffraction film to transform ordinary fluorescent lamps into objects that glow with an array of colours. Her Wonderfluoro lights look different from every angle.
rachelharding.co.uk

Photo Maris Mezulis

Commissioned by the city of Paris, Archiee and Sinato drew an illuminated colour-changing veil of haze over the interior of a pedestrian tunnel for climate-themed arts festival La Nuit Blanche.
archiee.com
sinato.jp

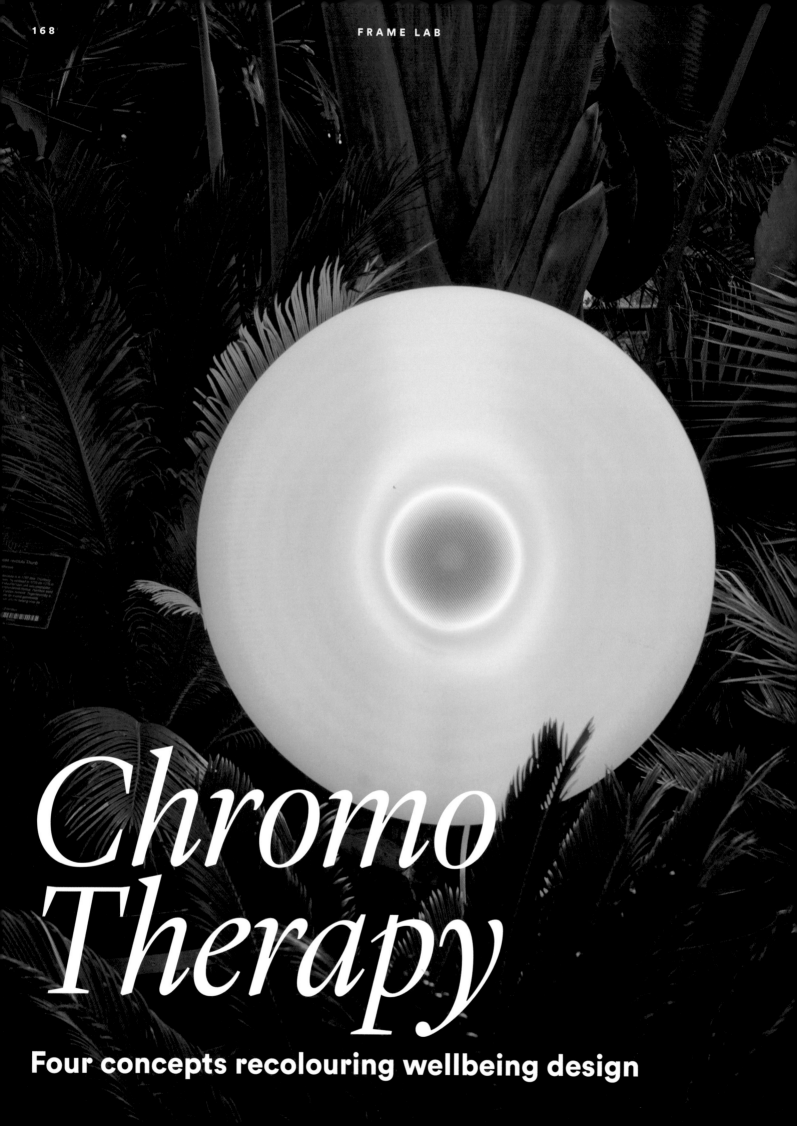

Chromo Therapy

Four concepts recolouring wellbeing design

1 restore

The remedial benefits of colour cater to our growing desire to take time out.

Studies show that pink is one of the most universally approachable colours and an outstanding example of the positive effect that 'physically soothing' hues can have on health and behaviour. In *Colour Psychology and Colour Therapy* (reprinted in 2013), colour psychologist Faber Birren writes of moving violent inmates into pink-painted prison cells to quell their aggressive behaviour. Pink surroundings have proved to be both effective and therapeutic, notwithstanding the 'girlie pink' stigma attached to the colour.

The growing preoccupation with personal wellness – illustrated in part by our increasing need to switch off and transcend the daily rush – is mirrored by a growing awareness of colour and its instrumental effect on mind, body and emotion.

Timely Colour

In an effort to achieve what he calls 'a more human time', Wout Wolf Stroucken designed O Clock, a mobile application and physical timepiece that use colour and motion to track the time. Unlike traditional clocks, which show what is to come and what has passed, O Clock displays only one hour at a time. 'For me, working with colours feels like a dialogue with the unconscious,' says the designer, who chose colours that feel 'most present' at certain times of day. 'Colours in the morning appear to be light, during the day saturated and in the evening warm.' He created each colour 'according to the moment'. ⤶

Pause, an app by Ustwo, acknowledges the value of personal taste as compared with predetermined perceptions of colour; users of Pause select colours based on their own preferences.

↰ Stroucken's approach to colour – very elemental, very intuitive – is a timely reminder that while the power of pink may have been medically verified, our very real connection with nature's daily cycle, as a source of peace and relaxation, remains without question.

Experiential App

Ignoring negative talk about the suppressing effect that blue light and LED screens have on our melatonin levels, design studio Ustwo went ahead and translated wellbeing and meditation into a digital experience that the makers claim has proved successful. Their app, Pause, encourages mindfulness through focused attention. Moving your finger across a screen that features graphics and colours reduces stress.

'We experimented a lot with a colourful yet soft illustration style,' says Jeremy Godefroid of Ustwo. 'We wanted colour to please and captivate the users' eyes in an app that lets them choose the colours themselves.' Blue suggests serenity, purple evokes spirituality and green conjures restfulness. Ultimately, though, beauty remains very much in the eye of the beholder. Godefroid, who realizes that some colours are associated with predetermined perceptions, says that 'we wanted to keep it open for all tastes'.

Deep Sleep

In the Chronarium, an immersive sleep laboratory by Loop.ph, two concepts form a union of colour, sound and light that elicits a 'restorative, calm and contemplative experience'. A combination of 'pink noise' (low-frequency sound that induces restful sleep) and a wash of coloured light helps to reset the sleeper's circadian rhythm and to generate a state of deep repose. Lying in a cosy hammock-like pod, the participant absorbs a 'soundtrack' of quieting influences designed to take him from consciousness to tranquil slumber. — AB

Inside the Chronarium, an immersive sleep laboratory conceived by Loop.ph, pink noise and coloured light help to reset the sleeper's circadian rhythm.

Photo James Fox

readjust

Chromatic lighting holds promise for travellers dealing with time zones and shifting periods of daylight.

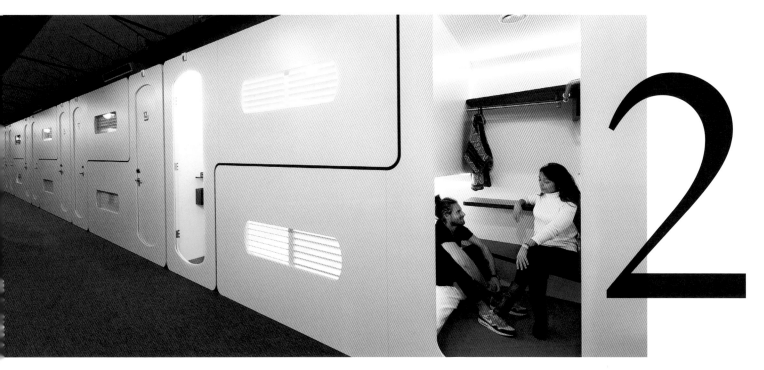

Equipped with adjustable mood lighting, CityHub's sleeping pods invite guests to personalize their space with the use of the accompanying app.

Travel has become part of everyday life. For some, it may be just a daily commute, but for others jet-setting is a fixture on the weekly agenda. Taking into account the move towards an increasingly nomadic lifestyle, Mariana Figueiro, program director at New York's Lighting Research Centre (LRC), points out the potential of light and colour for the hospitality industry in her webinar for Philips Lighting Academy. 'It can be very complicated for people to know when they need light and when they don't,' says Figueiro. 'We think the solution involves each individual having an app or circadian watch that beeps every time they need to change the light around them.' In terms of hospitality, Figueiro envisions an ideal model in which the infrastructure of a hotel allows guests to enter data from their sensors and let lighting do the rest. Figueiro imagines people on the go carrying a toolkit that includes various sleep masks and coloured glasses. By acknowledging the strains of jet lag and the pains of working to deadlines in different time zones, the model she proposes seems certain to make people not only healthier but more efficient as well.

Personal apps and watches are not the only aids designed to control the effects of light and colour on the human body. California start-up Ario is working along the same vein with Ario, its eponymous floor lamp. When connected to Wi-Fi, the smart lamp imitates the light of the sun and, in so doing, boosts the user's wellbeing. Similar to other Wi-Fi-enabled products – one example is Nest, a self-learning thermostat created by former Apple engineers – Ario monitors users' movements to achieve the colour and strength of light needed to optimize their health.

While items like Ario focus predominantly on the domestic enviroment, possibilities for their use in the contract sector are also being recognized. CityHub, a hostel in Amsterdam whose private sleeping cabins are a substitute for bedrooms, was designed by Studio Überdutch in collaboration with CityHub founders Sem Schuurkes and Pieter van Tilburg. Units cater to guests' preferences with a range of adjustable coloured lights that operate via an app. Although the result appears to be more about atmosphere – 'romance' and 'ocean' are among the options – than on wellbeing, lighting at CityHub does suggest a step towards a format compatible with LRC's research.

CityHub's sleeping pods and Ario's technology may reflect Figueiro's vision, but the 'potential' she mentions is still future-speak. Much of what is on the market today emerged from consumer demand rather than need – and on a call for ways to track an individual's movements to a particular location. A personal sensor with the capacity to tap into different infrastructures as we travel through time zones might raise the impact of colour and light on good health to the next level. Stay tuned to discover the first product to reach that height. — EM

detect

Smart technologies transform the body into a health-monitoring interface.

Googling has long been a popular form of self-diagnosis for anyone with a sniffle, a cough or a sore throat. Not much can be said for the accuracy of the findings though. Within the next decade, however, Dr Google's prognoses will be somewhat obsolete, having been replaced by sensor devices that read our numerous health and wellbeing signals and convey them to us through visual languages and universally understood communications systems, like colour-coding.

Diagnostic Aids

We're already seeing such aids emerge, thanks to technological developments and innovative designs. Developed by researchers at the University of Bath is a smart burns dressing that changes colour when a wound becomes infected. Toxic bacteria trigger nanocapsules within the dressing, which then release a fluorescent green dye. A team at the University of

Photo Mark Serr

Pennsylvania developed a colour-changing polymer crystal that promises to determine the severity of head traumas suffered by people wearing helmets while playing contact sports. Medical staff can ascertain instantly, by means of colour, the location and intensity of a blow involving headgear equipped with the polymer-based material.

Revealing Apparel

Giving more fashionable form to the idea of 'skin as interface' is designer-researcher Paulien Routs who – with Droog, Thewa Innovations, Annebeth Kroeskop and the Dutch Cosmetics Association – came up with sweat-sensitive textile coating Soak. Routs shifts the focus from health-related wearables that pit you against yourself (think Fitbit) to a more intimate type of wellness. Her aptly titled product analyses the composition of perspiration secreted by the person wearing a 'Soaked' outfit – particularly during periods of physical exercise – and, again with colour, reveals

the results. An intelligent colour system reads wearers' hydration levels as the coating reacts to the acidity in their sweat. Blue indicates a well-hydrated user, while hues from yellow to brown warn of dehydration. When the cause of dehydration is a poor diet, the warning might include information like 'too much coffee', shown by the colour brown.

Wary Wearable

One notable pioneer on the frontier of wearable monitoring devices is New Deal Design (NDD), the inventor of Sproutling, a sensor that tracks, among other things, a baby's sleep patterns. The soft anklet uses a smart charger and a mobile app to follow baby as she sleeps, wakes, fusses or lies calmly in her cot. An at-a-glance chromatic system calls attention to a possible fever with red, an unattached sensor with yellow, and so on. The next frontier, according to NDD, will see electronics embedded under the skin. — **AB**

New Deal Design also makes Fever Scout, a temperature-monitoring plaster with adhesive circuit technology from Vivalnk that connects to a smartphone app.

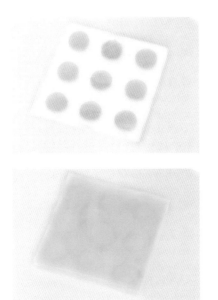

Scientists at the University of Bath developed burn dressings that contain nanocapsules, which release a fluorescent dye when wounds becomes infected.

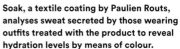

Soak, a textile coating by Paulien Routs, analyses sweat secreted by those wearing outfits treated with the product to reveal hydration levels by means of colour.

4

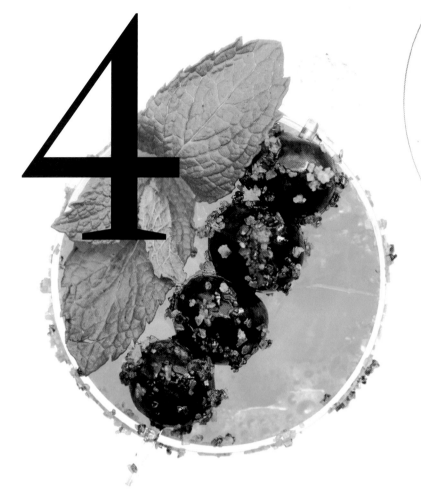

reconsider

A coloured pattern of dots on tableware by Studio José de la O suggests the right dietary portions of a meal.

Photo Dafne Ríos and Manuel Torres

Designers employ colour cues to alter food perception.

Would you consider taking a bite of a bright blue pizza or sipping a grey cocktail? A good appetite and unnatural colours rarely mix. Colour is closely related to the appeal of food and drink. It's the most important sensory cue for setting our expectations about taste before we dig in. The psychological impact that colour has on the perception of flavour makes it a powerful design tool.

Emotional Engagement

Palette for Your Palate, an online exhibition, is an inspirational example of the effect that colour has on mood. Vancouver outfit Tealeaves invited chefs and mixologists to develop recipes and cocktails based on three things: the brand's tea blends, matching colours picked by the Pantone Color Institute, and associated moods. The project explores the subconscious role colour plays in emotional engagement. 'Our reaction to colour is, for the most part, intuitive and emotional; only 5 per cent is rational,' says Pantone's Laurie Pressman in an interview posted on klad.com. Warm colours can evoke feelings of comfort or anger, while cool colours often generate calmness or sadness. Tealeaves' invitation resulted in drinks like Kevin Spicknell's

Photo ÉCAL/Axel Crettenand

Left **Tealeaves asked a group of culinary experts to create a dish or drink that would combine a tea blend with a Pantone colour and its associated mood.**

Peppermint Tea Margarita, a vibrant cocktail that references both the brand's Organic Peppermint Tea and a striking shade of blue: Pantone 290 C.

Tempting Tap Water

Focusing on the fusion of design and human behaviour, ÉCAL graduate Hansel Schloupt came up with Solid Syrup to make the idea of drinking water appealing to children. To do so, he borrowed colour-based design strategies used to make soft drinks irresistible and applied them to water. Kids can see Schloupt's syrup – made of dehydrated fruit powder – dissolve as it turns clear water into different colours; at the same time, they view the relationship between colour and taste.

Influential Tableware

Creative agency Studio José de la O takes the notion of stimulating yet healthy choices a step further with Portion Distortion, a conceptual set of dinnerware that examines how product design influences eating patterns. The studio's plates and bowls feature dotted patterns in different colours, which indicate wholesome portions of protein, veg and carbs. These visual guidelines not only demonstrate how much the user should eat but also have the potential to enhance flavour: according to research done at the University of Oxford, colour used in the design of a bowl can elicit perceptions of sweetness or saltiness. — KvdM

Hansel Schloupt's Solid Syrup comes as tablets of dehydrated fruit powder; the designer borrowed colour-based strategies used in the soft-drink industry for his healthier alternative.

In Limbo, a series of distorted portraits by
Emon Toufanian, depicts warped psyches.
e m o n . n y c

OFF

Counterbalancing today's constant pursuit of happiness, designers revalue the darker emotional states, which prove to be just as important.

WORDS *Floor Kuitert*

colour

Commissioned by New Window, Rop van Mierlo
layered the seven colours of the rainbow on top
of one another and in different orders to achieve
Black Rainbow, an extremely colourful yet dark
limited edition of photographic prints.
ropvanmierlo.nl

EMOTION has become inextricably linked to design. Terms like 'the experience economy' and 'mindfulness' have crept into our creative vocabularies and seem here to stay. Transcending purely functional and aesthetic purposes, design is expected to offer something more. Like art, it should 'touch' us, evoke feelings and engender emotional responses.

Naturally, makers and storytellers aim for positive sensations. As a result, joy and happiness dominate today's visual and vocal communication culture. Brands want clients to feel a warm sense of belonging, and to achieve that goal they use pleasant, welcoming sounds and images. But just how realistic is this strategy? Yes, people are social beings, but not 24/7.

Equally important is the growing desire to get closer to oneself. To turn inwards and discover the core of your being 'for better *or* worse'. Like the seasons, we tend to have darker periods in our lives, during which gloom and melancholy overpower us and emotional lows outnumber euphoric highs. And that's *okay*. Embracing a wide spectrum of emotions creates a healthy, balanced mind.

Swiss psychoanalyst Carl Jung wrote that 'everyone carries a shadow', in reference to a person's unconscious, usually negative side. But he also wrote that 'in spite of its function as a reservoir for human darkness – or perhaps because of this – the shadow is the seat of creativity.'

We can conclude that Jung wanted us to accept solitude and introversion and that he encouraged the human mind to wander. Certain spaces, designs and pieces of art support rituals that accompany sadness and despair. Some offer users tools for contemplation or unhurried activity: a place for ponderous pacing while becoming lost in thought.

An ominously apocalyptic vibe penetrates contemporary imagery and gives shape to previously undervalued moods. Glitches and noise suffuse work in which decay and transience are recurring themes, while dark and saturated colours make for sombre viewing. Take a leap in the dark. ✖

Based on research into rituals of loss and sadness, designer Nel Verbeke's Embrace Melancholy is a set of tools that enables users to experience and accept depression.
nelverbeke.com

Portuguese designer Giestas created
Soft Colour Emotions II, a visual diary
of his colour-coded emotions, both
experienced and expressed. Blues
represent the more melancholic days.
g i e s t a s . c o m

Photo Timothy Saccenti

Aptly titled *Struggle Sessions*, a zine by Timothy Saccenti and Sam Rolfes, with designs by Build, features portraiture that 'explores the deconstruction of the human form'.
timothysaccenti.com
samrolfes.com

'*Everyone carri*

The black cloud in *Becoming Wilderness
XXVIII* (2015) 'works as an act of violence
on the generic sunset photograph',
explain makers Inka and Niclas.
i n k a a n d n i c l a s . c o m

rries a shadow'

'Though the source material for these images is terrestrial, the photographs depict a fabricated place – a landscape of the mind,' says photographer CJ Heyliger about *Hell Mirage*, an ongoing series that includes *Sun Drip*.
cjheyliger.com

For his Flora collection, Marcin Rusak (*Frame* 101,
p. 076) encased discarded flowers in black resin.
Cutting the material reveals petals embedded inside.
m a r c i n r u s a k . c o m

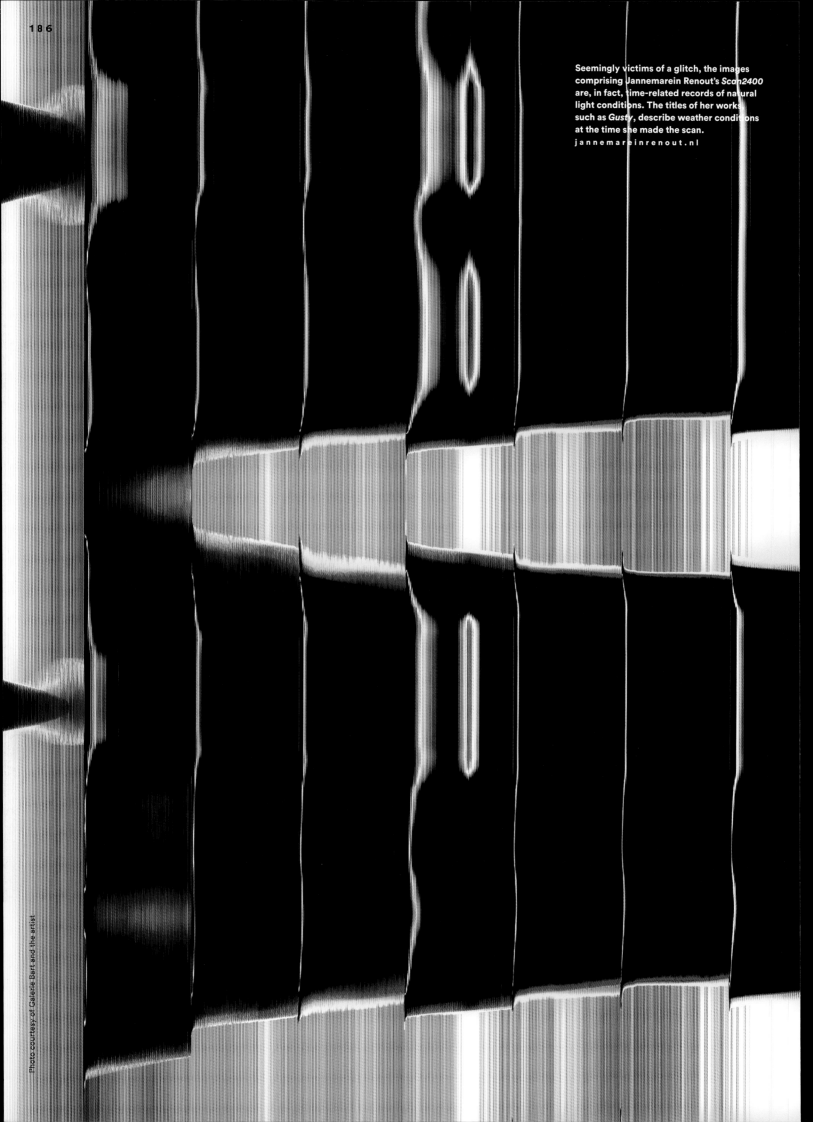

Seemingly victims of a glitch, the images comprising Jannemarein Renout's *Scan2400* are, in fact, time-related records of natural light conditions. The titles of her works such as *Gusty*, describe weather conditions at the time she made the scan.
j a n n e m a r e i n r e n o u t . n l

Photo Valeriane Lazard

DAE's Charlotte Jonckheer chose black for Pas Pardus, a rug designed for pacing back and forth while waiting. Because black absorbs light, we notice the various textures of the tufted rug only by walking on it barefoot.
charlottejonckheer.com

space & interiors
by MADE expo

architectural details

space&interiors is an exciting event put together by the MADE expo team for professionals heading to Design Week 2016 in search of cutting edge architectural finishes to enhance their projects

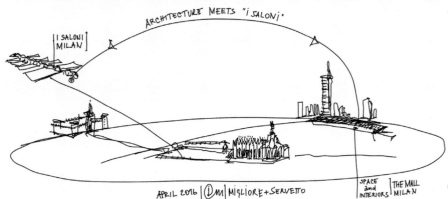

Architecture links up with the Salone del Mobile.Milano

space&interiors is the only event that's been given the nod to link up with Milan's world famous furniture show, including via visitor-only shuttle buses running between the two venues

A PIONEERING FORMULA CENTRED ON ARCHITECTURAL FINISHES

Curated by Migliore + Servetto Architects, the **advanced-concept display space** will give visitors an **immersive multisensory experience**. Besides delivering world class trade offerings, the event will also stage the **New Components Code** exhibit, designed to give the products an emotional rendering. A collection of the finest interior design materials of today and tomorrow

AN EXCLUSIVE LOUNGE AREA

Operators and trade visitors can use the exclusive lounge area for business meetings or to relax and take part in the glamour of Design Week

THE PRODUCTS

Surfaces, floorings, wall coverings, colour and decoration, doors, door handles, finishes, shelving, staircases, architectural glass, façade and cladding materials, windows and glazing, pergolas, gazebos, awnings, architectural lighting, Domotics, home automation and home entertainment

THE FIRST PARTICIPATING EXHIBITORS

3A Composites, Assa Abloy Italia, Bianchi Lecco, Dierre, Effeitalia, Fantoni, Garofoli, Gypsum, In Sinergia Contract, Italserramenti, Knauf Amf Italia, Legnoform, Manital, New Design Porte, Oikos Venezia, Okey, Ponzio, Salice Paolo, Secco Sistemi, System, Tabu, Velux, Virag

AN EVENT THAT'S NOT TO BE MISSED!

**Milan, Design Week
Piazza Lina Bo Bardi**

space-interiors.it

Brera
DESIGN DISTRICT MILANO

Outdoor

Kettal stamps out the latest in aluminium technology. **Moroso**, **Dedon**, **Extremis**, **Deesawat** and **Vondom** gather, play and relax. **B&B Italia**, **Paola Lenti** and more plump up the volume, while **Knoll**, **Estudio Campana** and others slim down.

Press,

Weighing less than 5 kg, Stampa has a delicate aluminium shell resting on slender legs. The design is a clever combination of high and low tech.

Puncture,

Kettal's Stampa reveals the latest in aluminium technology: the transformation of sheet metal into a cool perforated 'textile' for warm days.

WORDS *Adrian Madlener*

Perch

WITH its mind set on producing a design classic, Spanish outdoor-furniture brand Kettal joined forces with French duo Ronan and Erwan Bouroullec for the company's latest offering: Stampa. The outdoor chair pushes the properties of aluminium, thanks to a cutting-edge technology that transforms sheet metal into a material with an openwork design. Durable yet delicate, the chair has a duality that doesn't stop there. 'The idea was to make a comfortable, long-lasting chair that couldn't be copied,' says Ronan Bouroullec. 'Stampa had to be both charming and calm.' With a vote of confidence from Kettal, the

1

Early concept sketches of Kettal's Stampa emphasize the chair's fluid form. Charged with the task of creating a 'classic', Ronan and Erwan Bouroullec set out to design an aluminium chair that could not be copied.

2

The result of a five-year collaboration between Kettal and the Bouroullec brothers, Stampa has a delicate sturdiness born of their exploration of material constraints. A miniature model displays Stampa's distinctive openwork design.

'The idea was to make a comfortable, long-lasting chair that couldn't be copied'

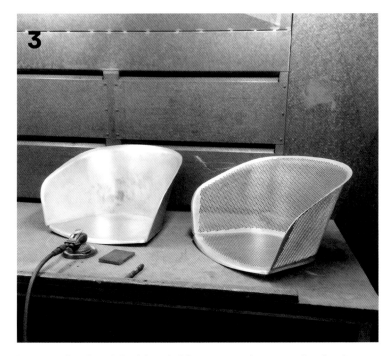

3

Stampa's calyx-shaped aluminium shell features a regular pattern of perforations.

4

An injection-moulded ring connects Stampa's seat to its back and armrests, and hydroformed legs support the shell.

brothers discovered the Barcelona brand's willingness to face new obstacles. Their five-year collaboration involved countless tests and experiments. 'Our in-house team gave 120 per cent to the development of Stampa,' says second-generation Kettal director Alex Alorda. 'Every modification was a challenge that we loved.' The family-run company's expertise in aluminium reaches back five decades: 'My father started working with the material in 1966. It has since become part of our DNA.'

The chair's unified aesthetic arises from the exploration of material constraints. Consisting of a combination of skilled craftsmanship and sophisticated manufacturing techniques, Stampa involves six procedures. 'It may not seem like it,' says Ronan, 'but the chair is a pressed, punched piece of flat metal, stamped and welded to form a calyx-shaped shell.' Stampa's core is held in place by an injection-moulded seat ring that is attached to hydroformed legs. A laser cutter punctures the sheet metal, and matching holes drilled by hand connect the perforated shell to the outer edge of the seat. A clever mix of high and low tech, Stampa's pierced shell not only helps keep it

– and the sitter – cool on warm days, but also makes the chair extremely lightweight.

Both the Bouroullecs and Kettal hope that the chair will gain value with use, stand the test of time, and become a classic. 'In 20 years, we'd like to find Stampa for sale at flea markets,' says Ronan. By opting for aluminium over plastic, the brothers aimed to extend the life of the outdoor chair. 'We wanted to emulate the longevity of repainted cast-iron garden furniture. We grew up in the countryside, and a harmonious landscape is very important to us.' ✕

kettal.com

Thin *or*

Slender silhouettes and full-figured forms take over the outdoor furniture scene this summer, offering choices for everyone.

Verena Hennig's Roll seating features rotatable aluminium tubes that massage the user's bottom and back for added comfort.
verenahennig.com

Photo Tilman Weishart

The motif for Estudio Campana's laser-cut Estrela collection is a pattern of stylized sand dollars.
campanas.com.br

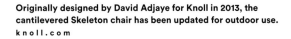

Originally designed by David Adjaye for Knoll in 2013, the cantilevered Skeleton chair has been updated for outdoor use.
knoll.com

Thick

Photo Sergio Chimenti, courtesy of Paola Lenti

Flexible straps facilitate the easy removal and storage of sausage-like backrest cushions, which highlight Patricia Urquiola's Roll collection for Kettal.
k e t t a l . c o m

Materials used to make the rotund Otto sofa, part of a series of the same name from Paola Lenti, are polystyrene (upholstery) and polyester fabric (cover).
p a o l a l e n t i . i t

Supported by a built-in metal frame, Patricia Urquiola's Fat-Sofa Outdoor for B&B Italia features an elegant woven structure that combines backrest and armrests.
bebitalia.com

Time Out

Top furniture brands enhance three veins of outdoor living.

WORDS *Jane Szita*

Doble, Hendrik Steenbakkers' table for Fueradentro, comes in various lengths – up to 2.7 m – and in three sleek finishes: Belgian bluestone, teak and toughened matte glass.

1

Gather

Socializing outdoors is the new cocooning.

We seem to be getting serious about entertaining outdoors, as demonstrated by a fresh range of alfresco dining solutions from furniture manufacturers. Belgian company Extremis breathes new life into an outdoor classic, the picnic table, adapting it for today's hyper-hospitable host in the form of a slightly surreal, extra-long version. The one-piece Marina picnic table and bench is made from a super-strong yet lightweight composite of fibreglass and polyester. Theoretically, this material makes the table virtually unlimited in length and able to seat up to 40 people, if you opt for the 12-m-long version. Its strong contemporary good looks come courtesy of design studio Fattorini+Rizzini+Partners.

A remake of the traditional root cellar, Weltevree's Groundfridge offers a sustainable way to store food and drink.

The growth in outdoor dining calls for new solutions in food-related facilities

The sunbed, too, gets a sociable makeover by Thai company Deesawat, which specializes in stylish and sustainable teak furniture. A fun variation on the archetypal one-person sun lounger, the Double Layer Bed consists, as the name suggests, of twin teak beds of different heights, partly upholstered in hardwearing fabric and resting on stainless-steel legs. Together, they comprise a versatile piece of furniture: part sunbathing deck, part lounge platform. It's a place for more than just resting, and unlike the traditional sunbed, it insists on being shared.

FueraDentro's stylish Doble, by Dutch designer Hendrik Steenbakkers, helps move the outdoor dining table in a new direction, as eating outside discovers its formal, as well

as casual, side. Tabletops in a variety of sizes – up to an expansive 2.7 m – come in several sleek finishes: Belgian bluestone, teak and toughened matte glass. The adjustable feet are in polished stainless steel. Versatility is key: the Doble table was designed with both modern and more traditional outdoor settings in mind, and it pairs easily with FueraDentro's Sillón or Butaque dining chair, as well as the matching Doble bench.

Naturally, the growth in outdoor dining also calls for new solutions in food-related facilities. One of the most innovative ideas, Weltevree's subterranean Groundfridge, actually harks back to the days of underground 'ice houses'. Organic and globe-shaped, manufactured in polyester

with a flight of stairs and a hatch at the top, Groundfridge is an off-the-grid solution that needs no electricity. Using the insulating capacity of the soil, it keeps the temperature a steady 10 to 12°C throughout the year, which is perfect for storing fruit, vegetables, wine and cheese. Its size (the equivalent of 20 standard refrigerators) makes it ideal for those who grow their own food.

Being outside no longer means roughing it, as outdoor lounge furniture leaves behind its Spartan past in favour of indulgent levels of comfort designed to ensure that guests will want to linger. Belgian company Manutti, for example, channelled the current trend for plump overstuffed seating into Kumo. The Japanese word for ↳

Envisioned as 'an evolution of the ancient fireplace that warms, entertains and feeds', Francesca Lanzavecchia and Hunn Wai's sustainable all-in-one Sunplace is a seating and table collection that harnesses solar power and employs a glass lens to cook food on a steel grill. To be a success, cooking with sunshine requires teamwork.

Photo Angelo Becci

cloud, *kumo* suggests the product's soft upholstery and lightness of design. A choice of modules invites customization. The user crafts a 'personalized outdoor cocoon' thanks to interchangeable covers in different shapes and sizes; decorative pillows, seat and back cushions; and an extensive range of fabric options.

Gloster's Grid is another example of an outdoor sofa system with an indoor level of comfort. It combines a cosy-but-clean lounge aesthetic with a super-flexible format. Designed by Henrik Pedersen, the seating has powder-coated-aluminium frames whose graphic lines are softened by generously upholstered cushions in neutral tones. 'A major leap forward in outdoor living comfort is in the textile area,' says Pedersen. 'With new yarns and coatings, we can now achieve almost the same results as those possible with indoor fabrics: a blend of comfort, expression and texture.' A range of coordinating tables with warm teak tops adds to the feel of the outdoor living space generated by Grid.

Lou, a modular lounge system designed by Toan Nguyen for German brand Dedon, was conceived as a series of overlapping horizontal strata. A curved module – a first for the company – gives the set a casual, friendly look; allows for rounded corners and semicircular arrangements; and naturally boosts social interaction. The seemingly light and effortless design introduces a new, semiopen variation on Dedon's trademark weave, which comes in several sophisticated shades of grey. Cushions ensure comfort but are thin and portable enough to be moved inside when a shower threatens to spoil the fun.

Whatever the weather, Ke Italy's Gennius and Xtesa shades promise protection from the elements and thus an extension of time spent outdoors together. The first is a series of modular sun-screening shelters whose folding awnings cover large areas. It has guttering to carry away rain and an optional hood with high thermic and acoustic insulation, making Gennius suitable for year-round use. Among the 24 models are those with traditional timber frames and others with modern aluminium frames. Xtesa is a streamlined, more compact solution with no crossbar. It has an electronically controlled shade and is wind- and water-resistant.

Another take on sociable shelter is Escofet's Domus, by Ramón Úbeda and Otto Canalda. A one-piece covered bench that looks like a little house, Domus relies on Escofet's UHPC concrete technology. It's both seat and refuge from the rain. 'Lightness and subtlety have triumphed over stiffness and weight,' says Escofet's Enric Pericas of the new material. In any case, the suggestive design is a guaranteed talking point intended to 'stimulate exchange and enrich interaction among users'. ↳

With a focus on flexibility and customization, Manutti's Kumo collection provides users with a choice of modules and covers that invites endless customization.

Grid, a flexible modular sofa designed by Henrik Pedersen for Gloster, carries the comforts of the living room out to the patio.

2
Relax

Dedon's MBrace, a design by Sebastian Herkner, is a fusion of fibres in warm, relaxing hues developed in collaboration with colourist Giulio Ridolfo.

Made of solid cedar, Riva 1920's Outdoor series develops a weathered finish over time.

Kicking back gets sophisticated.

↰ Enticing the user to stretch out and rest, if not sleep, Nardi's Atlantico sunbed is devoid of sharp corners, has a low-key matte finish and, in the words of designer Raffaello Galiotto, 'moulds softly to the user's body with a friendly attitude'. In other words, it exemplifies the current wellness aims of outdoor furniture. As Nardi CEO Floriana Nardi puts it: 'Outdoor settings are increasingly becoming a significant venue dedicated to rest and recuperation, where body and mind retrieve their balance, in contact with the natural elements.'

Relaxed and rounded forms make Vondom's newly extended UFO collection, by Ora-Ïto, an ambient addition to any space devoted to relaxation. The designer points out that its restful effect, which comes from a balance of contrasting positive and negative forms, was inspired by sculptor Martha Pan, whose work 'encourages relaxation and comfort' through its concern with symmetry, balance and geometry.

Retro style is key to the laid-back aesthetic of Royal Botania's New England collection by Pierre Stelmaszyk. Based on the Adirondack chair, originally designed by Thomas Lee in 1903 for his summer house in Westport, New York, the collection updates the American classic by 'making it more aesthetically balanced and enhancing the functionality and level of refinement, without disavowing its roots'. Available in teak or painted red or white, the armchairs make a comfortingly familiar statement while offering a relaxing seat.

Riva 1920's Outdoor collection of simple forms in solid cedar illustrates a relaxed approach to natural weathering: the small stools and tables are designed to wear with the elements, eventually becoming dove-grey and developing a unique patina, depending on where they are placed. Hand-finished and elemental in design, these pieces evoke driftwood on a beach and suggest timelessness and ↳

Marc Thorpe's Husk chair for Moroso was inspired by the outer leaves of an ear of corn. A curved backrest towers over the seat to shield its occupant from the outside world.

Photo Klára Dlouhá

Designed to facilitate relaxation and meditation, Swingy by Czech designer Linda Vrnáková features therapeutic massage balls covered in a durable fabric. 'The main reason I created Swingy was to help me meditate,' says Czech designer. 'The hammock's swaying motion has a positive effect on both body and mind. It boosts the imagination and promotes relaxation.'

A design by Patrick Norguet for Ethimo, the Swing sofa has a delicate framework in solid teak.

Outdoor lounge furniture leaves behind its Spartan past in favour of indulgent levels of comfort

Devoid of sharp corners, Nardi's compact Atlantico sunbed was designed by Raffaello Galiotto with urban dwellers in mind.

↰natural processes – adding an element of contemplation to the outdoors.

Moroso's Husk by Marc Thorpe is similarly inspired by nature, in this case by fields of corn in Northern Italy, particularly those close to the city of Udine. He translated the architecture of the husk of an ear of corn to produce a chair that effectively shields the user from the outside world without excluding it completely. Part of Moroso's M'Afrique collection, Husk is manufactured in Dakar, Senegal, and comes in three colours – red, green and white – and in three heights.

Patrick Norguet's Swing collection for Ethimo is a set of finely detailed pieces that exude a soothing repetition of teak slats together with aluminium components to add a nestlike feel to the system. The Swing seat has a dual structure: an external metal frame

is wrapped in a sail through which daylight filters to those tucked inside – the absolute height of cosiness

Dedon's Tigmi by Jean-Marie Massaud takes a comparable micro-architectural approach, combining the feel of being outdoors with that of being inside. A wide sofa with an optional 'roof', Tigmi merges seating and shelter, providing both shade and privacy. The atmosphere is reminiscent of a beach hut, but double layers of cushions ensure optimal comfort. Dedon's MBrace, designed by Sebastian Herkner, utilizes another innovative application of the company's woven material, this time a fusion of three separate fibres in warm shades developed with prominent colourist Giulio Ridolfo. The name MBrace comes from the snug bucket shape of the chair, which rests on a solid teak base.

3
Play

Thonet's All Seasons collection sends designs by Mart Stam, Marcel Breuer and Ludwig Mies van der Rohe into the wild.

Perfect for children and the young at heart, Gandiablasco's Tipi is a minimalist tent for outdoor adventures.

Fun, fantasy and freedom thrive in the great outdoors.

Psychological studies show that being outside boosts creativity, so it's hardly surprising when manufacturers appeal to our playful side with outdoor pieces intended to stimulate the imagination. When Dirk Wynants designed Walrus for Extremis, he had poolside and all-weather fun in mind. A comfortable seating system with deceptive good looks, Walrus sports a super-robust, water- and weather-proof upholstery fabric. A highlight is the concealed storage pouch, which contains a fold-out blanket and a thick cushion – offering a warm, dry place to perch whatever the circumstances.

A summer cocktail party sparked the design of Emu's Kira collection, by Christophe Pillet. The range of chairs and footrests matches aluminium tubing with a lightweight high-tech fabric tough enough for outdoor use. Available in several colourways, the semitransparent surfaces of Kira's seats and stools reveal their structural contours, for a provocative touch to Pillet's airy simplicity.

A playful approach to the classics makes iconic designs by Mart Stam, Marcel Breuer and Ludwig Mies van der Rohe fresh additions to outdoor life in Thonet's All Seasons collection. In lightweight weather-resistant mesh with power-coated-aluminium frames, revered designs like Mies's cantilever chair S 533 are now available in numerous fully customizable combinations: mix and ↳

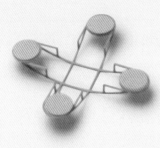

Loose Play, Capucine Diancourt's collection of playground equipment, was designed as a rejection of strict health and safety regulations. The objects rest on curved bases that rock back and forth, making them perilously difficult to balance on – which is all part of the fun, of course.

'Outdoor furniture design has for too long been constrained by what is practical and economical. Concept-style outdoor furniture is finally coming to the fore'

BEAU SPINKS, TIIPII

Trotter, a mobile chair by Rogier Martens for Magis, encourages children to engage in physical activity outdoors.

An integrated storage pouch makes Extremis's water- and weather-proof Walrus sofa practical and fun.

↰match their bright, contemporary colours with a series of frames in different forms.

Rogier Martens' Trotter, a mobile children's chair for Magis, comprises steel tubing and a rotation-moulded wheel. Shaped like a wheelbarrow, Trotter 'is specifically made to increase children's active experiences', says Martens. 'The wheel makes it possible to move the chair in an easy, playful way.'

Also for children are Ágatha Ruiz de la Prada's whimsical 'mini' pieces for Vondom. The Agatha collection is composed of a flower-shaped table and a heart-shaped chair. Featuring candy colours and textures, Agatha is hard-wearing and practical, as well as highly decorative, even when not in use by the little ones.

Adults as well as kids love TiiPii, a bed from the Australian company of the same name. Weighing only 4 kg and packing into a small bag, the circular bed hangs from a central point and can be installed quickly and comfortably. It accommodates two adults or up to five children. Says the company's Beau Spinks: 'Outdoor furniture design has for too long been constrained by what is practical and economical, but with advancements in engineering and manufacturing processes, we're finally able to bring concept-style outdoor furniture to the fore, and to enhance a space with pieces that represent a lifestyle

rather than simply being an application.'

Gloster's Voyager Deck Chair is a new take on a tried-and-tested outdoor staple – the deckchair. Inspired by campaign furniture popular in the colonial era, the Voyager Deck Chair combines contemporary good looks with a vintage flair, thanks to designer Povl Eskildsen's blend of buffed teak, seaside colours and clever powder-coated accents. Quick and easy to use, the space-saving design stores flat.

In the same vein, Kalon Studios reinvents the tripod campaign stool and calls it the Coyote. Part of Kalon's Wilderness Collection, Coyote lends an old classic a cool modern look that's at home just about anywhere. Style and simplicity go together

in this streamlined piece, with its tapered octagonal legs in solid ash and a seat cut from a single piece of leather. The all-natural, all-American product promises to age beautifully. A leather leash that ties the legs together makes Coyote easy to carry.

Who didn't love playing in a tent as a child? Tapping into that universal experience is Gandiablasco's Tipi, another example of learning from archetypes. The elegantly minimalist tent is made from anodized aluminium and plastic sheets in a wide range of textures and colours ideal for customization. Covering the floor is a small mattress filled with polyurethane foam; this and the accompanying cushions are available in different colours. ✕

From Poultry

Emilie van Spronsen converts diseased chicken carcasses into precious 'china'.

WORDS *Adrian Madlener*

Delft University of Technology graduate Emilie van Spronsen sterilized the bones of H5N8-infected chicken carcasses, making the remains suitable for reuse.

Opposite **Consisting of a mixture of bone ash and clay, the H5N8 Urn combines ceramics with 3D printing technology.**

Photos Anne Claire de Breij

To Porcelain

I N an effort to offset the immeasurable waste caused by the food industry's mishandling of an avian flu outbreak in the Netherlands, Delft University of Technology graduate Emilie van Spronsen sought to rectify the carnage with design. Her H5N8 project, aptly named after the virus, addresses overproduction and the poor treatment of livestock. Although more than 150,000 chickens were slaughtered at the time, an official confirmation of infection involved only four poultry farms.

Van Spronsen, who viewed the subsequent massacre of all poultry as a fundamental disregard for life, came up with an idea that expresses internationally recognized animal rights.

Experimenting with chicken bones, feathers and feet, Van Spronsen discovered that she could kill the virus by exposing the carcasses to a temperature of 70°C for at least three seconds, making the discarded chickens suitable for reuse. Once sterilized, fragments of the birds were used to make

a collection of household objects. Among them, the H5N8 Urn merges ceramics with 3D printing. Composed of a mixture of chicken-bone ash and clay, the vessel emulates the virus's microscopic cell structure. It also contains the bird's cremated remains, paying homage to the deceased while promoting new life: adding the ashes to arable soil contributes to healthier crops. The H5N8 Urn transforms what was once waste into a sustainable resource. ✕

emilievanspronsen.com

Crystal Clear

Snubbed by a Dutch glass manufacturer in the late 1970s, Gijs Bakker's visionary Tripod lamp withstands the test of time.

WORDS *Maria Elena Oberti*
ILLUSTRATION *Maiko Gubler*

Gijs Bakker

Born in Amersfoort, the Netherlands, in 1942, jeweller and industrial designer Gijs Bakker received his training at the Gerrit Rietveld Academie in Amsterdam and at Konstfack University College in Stockholm. The Dutchman cofounded Droog Design in 1993 and served as head of Design Academy Eindhoven's graduate department between 1987 and 2012. Bakker is the creative director of Han Gallery in Taiwan and of chp...? jewelry, a brand he established in 1996. He lives and works in Amsterdam, and his designs are exhibited in such prestigious venues as London's Victoria and Albert Museum, the Museum of Modern Art in New York City, the Helen Drutt Gallery in Philadelphia, and the Stedelijk Museum in Amsterdam.

Bakker's 1978 Tripod emerged from his design of Zaklampen, a lighting installation he'd completed earlier that year, which consisted of a succession of fluorescent elements covered in a translucent fabric. Inspired by the idea of using a single material, Bakker set out to design a lamp that would be 'as low tech as possible'.

In 1978 Bakker (left) presented a series of prototypes to Royal Leerdam's design director, Floris Meydam, one of which was the original design for Tripod.

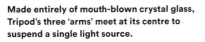

Made entirely of mouth-blown crystal glass, Tripod's three 'arms' meet at its centre to suspend a single light source.

'Something becomes iconic when it is the clearest execution of a concept'

' T H E first time I came across Tripod was when I visited Gijs at his home in Amsterdam. We were sitting around his dining table, having tea and talking, and in the far corner was this glass lamp,' says Christian Elving, CEO of Danish homeware brand Lyngby Porcelain. Gijs Bakker originally designed Tripod for Dutch glass manufacturer Royal Leerdam. He presented the concept to the company's design director, Floris Meydam, in early October 1978. Despite Meydam's enthusiasm, conflicting interests within the company prevented the lamp from going into production. Captivated by the simplicity of Bakker's vision, Elving was determined to resurrect Tripod as part of his collection of glass and porcelain products.

'I was baffled by the idea of hanging a bulb in midair. It's such a clear and strong

concept,' Elving tells me over the phone. The lamp is made entirely of highly transparent, quality crystal glass, resulting in an object of extreme luminosity. Three 'arms' meet at the centre of a dome to suspend a single 'floating' light source. 'It's a beautiful image,' says Elving. 'I love the way the light interacts with the crystal and casts shadows.'

The first of a 'catalogue' of proposals, Bakker's concept for Tripod was triggered by a lighting installation he'd completed earlier that year entitled Zaklampen, which consisted of a succession of fluorescent elements clad in a translucent fabric. Bakker took the same minimalist approach when responding to Royal Leerdam's invitation. 'It was the first time I had worked with glass. I wanted to escape from technical solutions and make something really low tech,' explains

Bakker from his canalside studio and home. Intent on using a single material, he set out to find the most straightforward way to achieve his goal. 'A lamp is a functional object. I wanted to stress its functionality by making the combination of glass and electricity as natural as possible.'

Based on images of the initial prototype, the reissued Tripod combines traditional glass-blowing techniques with the accuracy of technology. A blowpipe is used to shape the piece in an upside-down wooden mould, and when the crystal is 'yellow hot', carbon rods crimp the dome on three sides to enhance the lamp's architecture. In 1978, special tools and artisanal expertise were needed for the rim and arms of the lamp. Today, machines take over. 'We came up with a device that allows us to make all three indentations at once. Another change is that we now cut the bottom of the glass, levelling the edges and making the sizes exact,' says Elving. Further improvements include a dimmer and a cloth-covered flex, which Bakker sees as 'elements of luxury'.

Elving cites three reasons for reissuing Tripod: 'It's timeless, beautiful, and iconic.' Bakker's tongue-in-cheek response? 'I only make iconic pieces,' he laughs. 'What makes a design iconic? That's a difficult question. I think something becomes iconic when it is the clearest execution of a concept.' Elving agrees. 'The genius of Tripod is the purity of the concept. You know exactly what it is when you look at it. There's no mistaking it for anything other than a lamp.' X

lyngbyporcelain.com
gijsbakker.com

Skin and Bone

Layer's Scale for Woven Image adapts to its environment to absorb sound

WORDS *Maria Elena Oberti*

2

connectors facilitate both straight and curved configurations

70

dB is the average volume of noise reduced

50

represents the percentage of hemp in each tile. The remaining materials are aluminium (10 per cent) and ABS (40 per cent)

3

is the number of materials used

5

prototypes and engineering steps were involved in reaching the final design

7 components clip together to make up each module

640

hours over two years went into developing the modular acoustic partition system